W9-ASP-715

ILLINOIS CENTRAL COLLEGE   2

A12901 372385

WITHDRAWN

VGM Opportunities Series

OPPORTUNITIES IN
FOREIGN LANGUAGE
CAREERS

Wilga M. Rivers

Revised by
Marguerite Duffy

Foreword by
C. Edward Scebold
Executive Director
American Council on the
    Teaching of Foreign Languages

VGM Career Horizons
NTC/Contemporary Publishing Group

P
60
.R5
1998

Library of Congress Cataloging-in-Publication Data

Rivers, Wilga M.
    Opportunities in foreign language careers / Wilga M. Rivers : rev.
by Marguerite Duffy.
      p.   cm. — (VGM opportunities series)
    Includes bibliographical references (p.   )
    ISBN 0-8442-6470-9. — ISBN 0-8442-6471-7 (pbk.)
      1. Language and languages—Vocational guidance. I. Duffy,
Marguerite. II. Title. III. Series.
P60.R5   1998
418'.0023—dc21   98-7380
                                                 CIP

Cover photo credits:
Images copyright © 1998 PhotoDisc, Inc.

Published by VGM Career Horizons
A division of NTC/Contemporary Publishing Group, Inc.
4255 West Touhy Avenue, Lincolnwood (Chicago), Illinois 60646-1975 U.S.A.
Copyright © 1999 by NTC/Contemporary Publishing Group, Inc.
All rights reserved. No part of this book may be reproduced, stored in a retrieval
system, or transmitted in any form or by any means, electronic, mechanical,
photocopying, recording, or otherwise, without the prior permission of NTC/
Contemporary Publishing Group, Inc.
Printed in the United States of America
International Standard Book Number: 0-8442-6470-9 (cloth)
                                     0-8442-6471-7 (paper)
18   17   16   15   14   13   12   11   10   9   8   7   6   5   4   3   2   1

CONTENTS

ABOUT THE AUTHOR

Wilga M. Rivers, Professor Emerita of Romance Languages and Literatures at Harvard University, received her Ph.D. from the University of Illinois at Urbana-Champaign, her M.A. from Melbourne University, a Licence des Lettres from the University of Montpellier (France), and an Honorary Doctor of Letters from Middlebury College. She has taught at the University of Illinois, Northern Illinois University, Monash (Australia), Columbia University, and Harvard University where she was Coordinator of Language Instruction. She has published numerous books on the theory and practice of language teaching, drawing insights from psychology and linguistics, with specific books on the teaching of French, German, Spanish, Hebrew, and English as a second or foreign language. She has lectured and taught courses and seminars in thirty-three countries and throughout the United States and Canada. Her books and articles have been translated into nine languages. During her career, Professor Rivers has taught students in elementary schools, high schools, universities, and adult education courses. One of her special interests has always been advising students on their careers and helping them find positions in the foreign language field that will bring them satisfaction.

This edition was revised by Marguerite Duffy, a veteran career writer and editor.

FOREWORD

Foreign languages are making the headlines again! We are experiencing a resurgence of interest in studying other languages. There has been extensive discussion of America's problem in competing in the international marketplace, of the need for persons with knowledge of second languages and cultures in key diplomatic and related government positions, and of the need for all Americans to have greater knowledge and appreciation of the languages and cultures of their neighbors, whether we speak of those down the block or neighbors on the other side of the globe.

To many, it may seem strange that knowledge of other languages continues to be a problematic issue for Americans. Others understand that history and well-established values stand in the way of finding a simple, short-term solution to America's lack of knowledge of second languages and lack of appreciation of the prerequisite for knowledge of a foreign language before any attempt is made to deal with the complex issues of our global society.

Those who read this new edition of *Opportunities in Foreign Language Careers* undoubtedly understand something of the subtlety and nuance of language and the depth and complexity of culture; what you seek at this point is specific advice and assistance on how to use the knowledge of a second language and culture in your professional life. Many will immediately find the help they want. Others will find that the answers to their questions are more complex. For example, second-language competence is not always recognized as a valuable commodity at entry-level positions by many corporations that deal extensively in international business; nonetheless, these skills may be the key stepping-stone to promotions or increased job responsibility. In other words, language competence may not get you the job, but it may be a key element in broadening the potential for growth and advancement once you are in the position. All those who are fluent in more than one language must keep in mind the long-term values and benefits of this knowledge.

Former United States Senator Paul Simon labeled us "tongue-tied Americans." You and others who have seen and appreciate the value of second-language competence are the link between today and tomorrow, a time when Americans may be known and recognized for their multilingual and multicultural abilities. Good luck in your search, and welcome to our shared challenge.

C. Edward Scebold
Executive Director
American Council on the
Teaching of Foreign Languages

CHAPTER 1

LOVE OF LANGUAGES:
THE FOREIGN LANGUAGE FIELD

As U.S. citizens have traveled more widely and many foreign students, businesspeople, and tourists have visited this country, Americans have become more aware of their general ignorance of other languages and cultures. They have seen their country's former economic and political dominance threatened by other countries that have been seizing the opportunities afforded by an ever-shrinking globe and the insatiable appetites of world markets. Americans also have been forced to recognize the many linguistic and cultural groups living together in this country, and they have begun to realize the need for greater understanding and acceptance of differences within their own communities. Many have become interested in finding out more about their own cultural origins, seeking information about their grandparents' countries of origin, cultural heritage, and values, and even trying to learn some of their language. Others have reclaimed the values of their precolonial ancestors. The greater American society has begun to recognize that it includes many different types of people whose words should be heard and whose contributions to literature, the arts, and the development of the nation should be acknowledged. This is reflected in the revised curricula in many areas of education, not only in languages.

From a low point in the 1970s and early 1980s, interest in learning languages gradually has grown, with an unusually sharp increase in Japanese and Chinese, whose importance had been overlooked in the past. Colleges have begun once again to require their students to demonstrate proficiency in another language; they also have tried to develop a more international attitude on the part of their students in many ways, including encouraging student exchanges and study abroad. Foreign language skills are important in many disciplines, including economics, history, and even engineering. According to statistics from the Modern Language Association, "in 1990 there were nearly 4.1 million students enrolled in foreign language classes in public high schools in the United States, 548,389 in public elementary schools, and nearly 1.2 million in colleges and universities. In short, about one of every five language students enrolled in language classes is studying at the college or university level."[1]

Foreign language programs once again are being established at the elementary school level, some of these programs practicing total immersion. Legislation has been passed by the United States Congress that would provide financial incentives for foreign language instruction and for study abroad. Foundations have been generous in funding language-related projects, like the establishment of the *National Foreign Language Center* at the Johns Hopkins University and the preparation of elaborate programs for learning languages through television. New developments like computer-assisted language learning, often with videodiscs that plunge the student deep into the life of the target language country, programs taken from satellite broadcasts, and modern links between classrooms here and abroad add a vivid new reality to language courses. The future for foreign language study seems much brighter, as language teachers realize that they have a much broader role to play in the educational process than they allowed themselves to envision in the not-so-distant past.

EMPLOYMENT OPPORTUNITIES

There is a wide range of jobs open to those possessing language competence, extending all the way from bilingual stenographer, clerk, or word processor, to the highly skilled interpreter at the United Nations or

---

[1]Richard D. Lambert, "Foreign Language Policy: An Agenda for Change," *The Annals of the American Academy of Political and Social Science,* vol. 532 (1994): 126.

the chief executive officer of a large company in the import-export trade. Positions are available at all levels of the business world, in teaching, government service, the health professions and social work, law enforcement, journalism, the travel and tourist industry, and international banking. From the Peace Corps volunteer and English teacher abroad to the fashion buyer, flight attendant, and agricultural specialist seeking to help a developing country, Americans are encountering situations everyday in which knowledge of another language can facilitate their work and make their contributions more effective.

The business world, export trade, international advertising, hotel and travel industries, and engineering construction in foreign countries are areas in which knowledge of another language is especially useful. However, it should be made very clear at the start that language is merely an additional asset in all these areas: the job itself requires technical or professional skill and knowledge.

In government, available situations are chiefly in foreign service. On the whole, they are interesting and remunerative and, in addition, provide opportunities for travel. The State Department employs many civilians abroad, and because of the role of the United States in world affairs and the ever-increasing number of new nations, the need for a large staff abroad undoubtedly will continue.

Many Americans find satisfying work in the Peace Corps and others in developing cultural programs and teaching their own language under the auspices of the United States Information Agency. Another government-supported area is that of bilingual education. This program, which is now widespread, offers many jobs in a variety of foreign languages at all school levels for those with native or near-native competence. The teaching of English and literacy skills to immigrants and migrants also brings the instructor into situations where knowledge of other languages can be an asset.

CAREER POTENTIAL

Peace, Paix, Paz, MNP: We have all received cards with intriguing multilanguage greetings like this, often illustrated with circles of people of very different physical appearance and dress, all holding hands and smiling. Such messages inspire us to communicate with other peoples, yet, the very next minute, we may see on the television news evidence of dreadful disunity and disharmony in many parts of the world, economic disintegration, and lack of adequate education and health services; we see people accustomed to traditional ways suddenly thrust into an increasingly complex and fast-moving international society. Surely something can be done, we think, to help people work together for the development of their local and national communities, integrating them into an enriching international environment. How can this be accomplished when so many people do not understand what others are saying or what their aspirations may be? We have also begun to realize that the welfare of our own community is interwoven with the greater good of communities far from our shores, even of some whom we scarcely knew existed until recently. Also overlooked are relations with minority groups in our own society. There is an urgent need for go-betweens in so many areas of international and national life—people who can build bridges of understanding and cooperation.

Just knowing another language, even enjoying it, is not enough. We must each earn a living, and your concern at this point is to find out whether there are careers open to you where your interest in other languages and cultures can be not only a personal satisfaction, but can lead to a satisfying vocation. In the following pages, we will try to help you develop personal answers by introducing you to various aspects of the foreign language field, so that you can better organize your preparation, and to vocations where your skills can be put to use. It will soon become apparent that language and cultural skills alone are not sufficient to develop a career. In each possible area of work, you must be fully qualified for the work itself—only then will your language and cultural skills emerge as an additional asset in your working environment. This applies even to areas of work that seem centered on language itself, such as language teaching (for which you must understand how to educate students, the ways in which people learn languages, and how to design a language program to meet students' objectives while enriching the wider curriculum within the school) or translating and interpreting (where familiarity with quite specialized fields of knowledge and human interaction is essential if you are to transmit meanings accurately).

First let us deal with several of your more burning and immediate questions before you begin consideration of career possibilities.

LEVEL OF LANGUAGE SKILL

What level of language skill should I aim for to use the language for career purposes? Even an elementary competence can be of some use in later life, if maintained. In a business career, it can help you oil the wheels of social contact and give pleasure to your counterparts who speak the language, as evidence that you come to them in an attitude of good will. It must, however, be accompanied by an appreciation of cultural differences and expectations. In social service careers, an elementary competence may help you to put clients who speak that language at ease, although it will usually not be sufficient for your professional work in meeting their needs. For language to be of value for career purposes, however, you will need to be able to understand a professional level of discourse, in all probability read letters, reports, and documents, and be able to express yourself clearly in professional interactions. For this you will need an advanced level of language competence. The American Council on the Teaching of Foreign Languages (ACTFL) has drawn up guidelines explaining what you should be able to do at four levels of competence, from Novice through Intermediate and Advanced to Superior. Your language instructor may be able to give you a copy of these guidelines, or you can write to ACTFL at the address given in Appendix A. Aim toward the Advanced Plus or preferably the Superior level by the end of your studies, or through your own efforts at a later date, always remembering that real language competence includes sociocultural and pragmatic competence, which we now will discuss.

CULTURAL UNDERSTANDING

Does using someone else's language accurately ensure understanding and cooperation? Let us first dispel any illusion that cross-linguistic understanding is a matter of knowing vocabulary and grammar rules and being able to string together meaningful, correctly formulated sentences. Each language brings along with it its individual culture—its set of expectations, its value system, and its ways of behaving in interaction with others. Consequently, what we should be aiming at, in perfecting our knowledge of another language, is an understanding of the ways in which it is used by its native speakers in particular situations to establish desired relationships; we will want to interact with them comfortably, without offending in subtle ways or disconcerting them with unexpected behavior. For this we will need to recognize nuances of expression that extend beyond mere formulation of phrases to appropriate physical behavior (body language, bowing, shaking hands, embracing, maintaining eye contact or lack of it, respecting personal space, keeping silence, interrupting or not interrupting) and the ways in which a discourse is developed (what is said; what is left unsaid or implied; how conversational episodes are initiated, maintained, or concluded; how the speaker indicates that he or she is holding the floor; how to interrupt; the ways in which native speakers convey their approval or disapproval, their reservations, or their emotional involvement, much of this coming under the heading of sociocultural and pragmatic competence). If your language study has not included these aspects of cross-cultural communication, you will need to develop your knowledge and sensitivity in such areas. When you have acquired a theoretical understanding of what to look for, carefully observe the interactions of any native speakers you meet or see in films or on television; this will help you to supplement your knowledge and develop some competence in these areas.

In a survey of "The Foreign Language Needs of U.S.-Based Corporations," Fixman (1990) discovered that "crosscultural understanding was viewed as important for doing business in a global economy,"[2] so proficiency in this area may be considered a career plus. As the career aspirant advances in the business world, it will become necessary to understand the corporate culture in different areas of the world (whether decisions are made immediately or after several days of apparently irrelevant social activities, whether it is or is not correct to read the small print before signing an agreement, whether one's word or a handshake is considered as binding as a signature, and so on); at this stage experience

---

[2]C. S. Fixman, in *Foreign Language in the Workplace,* eds. R. D. Lambert and S. J. Moore (Newberry Park, CA: Sage Publications, 1990), pp. 25–46.

in observing and analyzing subtle cultural differences and signals will prove an invaluable asset.

When you use a language outside of a classroom, you will find that there are dialectical differences and various degrees of formality and informality; sometimes there will be differences in language addressed to or used by men and women or in speaking with persons of different levels of authority or subordination. Furthermore, for the language to be generally useful to you, you will need to practice listening to different types of voices, to persons from different regions and levels of society in various relationships. These may not have been central to the rather neutral presentation of your language class. You must work toward a period of residence in an area where the language is spoken. Essentially you must learn to use a language in all its fullness by developing an awareness of what you can teach yourself. This ability to learn autonomously will serve you well in your career, especially if your work requires you to use a different language than the one you have already acquired.

WHICH LANGUAGE WILL YOU NEED?

What if the language I have been learning in high school or have continued to learn in college is not the one I will need in my career? This appears to be a greater problem than it is. When we learn a language, no matter which one, we learn how languages work and that they frequently work in quite different ways from our native language. We also learn how to learn a language, and experience has shown that this makes the learning of further languages easier as we go along. If we have learned one of the languages in common use for international communication, this will serve us in good stead in all kinds of situations, even if it is not the language we most need for career purposes (among such languages we can list English, French, German, and Spanish). We learn these languages, not merely so that we can communicate with native speakers, but also to socialize and conduct business with people worldwide who speak these languages. If you have already decided that you will seek a career in which languages are important, then try to acquire a second foreign language while you are still in school or college, particularly one that seems to have applications for the career you have in mind. Alternatively, in order to broaden your experience with languages, begin to study one that operates completely differently from your first foreign and native languages and that brings you into contact with a culture and institutions very different from your own. Later, when your career path is clearer, your employing agency will see that you have opportunities for intensive study of a needed language, and your experience in language learning will pay off.

Finally, if you have acquired a language bilingually in the home, take great care not to let it atrophy. If possible, take some advanced courses where you will need to use it—this will increase the sophistication of your control of it. You are fortunate in having a head start, and at some later date this may be the very thing that ranks you above other candidates for some job-related project.

CHOOSING A COLLEGE OR GRADUATE SCHOOL

What should I look for in choosing a college or graduate school? Look for a school that encourages an interdisciplinary approach to language study. Information and knowledge are being rapidly integrated, and one subject area now illuminates and enriches others. Unfortunately, many foreign language departments are set in old ways, seeing language only as a tool for studying literature or linguistics. Many professional schools have a narrow view of career preparation, not allowing credit for further language study. Once you have settled into a college, do not expect that you will be able to change attitudes; your department will expect you to conform to what they have always expected of students. Consequently, it is in your best interest to look ahead.

In selecting a college or graduate school, be sure to ask questions about the types of programs offered. It is important to know whether the foreign-language department offers a diversified major to accommodate students with different career goals. Do they offer, for instance, a language major with a minor or a double major in business, journalism, international affairs, the arts, or whatever interests you? If not, are there structures that will allow you to draw up a plan for a special concentration or minor for yourself, after consultation with the department, enabling you to take courses related to your interests in other departments? Alternatively, does the professional department of your career major (the school of business, government, or engineering, for instance) give credit for extra work in a language related to your career goals, or does it have links already established for cross-disciplinary double majors or minors?

In a number of schools there are isolated courses in Spanish for law enforcement or health personnel, in Italian for musicians, or French for architects. These may or may not be part of a career-oriented sequence. This should be checked out. Some colleges and universities do have special programs that recognize the importance of language as a career adjunct. At the University of Pennsylvania, the Wharton School's Lauder Institute of International Management requires high-level language skills for admission to graduate studies and incorporates the use of language in its courses on international business. For the master's degree at the Monterey Institute of International Studies, students must have completed the equivalent of five college-level semester courses in a language related to their special area of study, and they then participate in a series of courses taught entirely or partly in that language, in politics, government, management, and so on. (This institute offers master's programs in international business, international policy studies, international public administration, language teaching, and translation and interpretation.) At the undergraduate level, Earlham College, Brown University, the University of Minnesota, and St. Olaf College incorporate readings and discussion in particular languages into courses in philosophy, history, social and political sciences, or law. Stanford University has double undergraduate majors with German in the departments of economics, international relations, history, and engineering; and the French Studies Department at the University of Illinois at Urbana-Champaign has a similar double major arrangement with the Department of Business Administration. There are, of course, others, but such programs have to be sought out.

If you wish to develop near-native proficiency, a period of study or working abroad is essential. Does the college or university you are considering have a year-abroad program, preferably with a home-stay component, in the language you are interested in, or does it have established links with a reputable program in a sister institution? Does it arrange for an internship abroad in the area of your career interest? At Stanford University, for instance, internships abroad are arranged for double majors in German and engineering or social sciences.

Some language departments provide courses for students interested in international business careers. These courses should be looked at carefully. They fall into three categories. The first type we may call commercial language courses; in this case, instead of learning a general vocabulary, students are taught more technical terms (for contracts, mortgages, leasing, balance sheets, or leveraged buyouts, for instance) and are given some experience in writing business letters. These courses may be at the elementary level or even the intermediate level. The second type are courses in language for business, at the upper intermediate or advanced level, in which students learn how business is conducted in the target country, something of its distinctive organization and operations, with some explanation of its corporate culture. These courses often provide opportunities to gain certificates of competence in business from the country concerned, as, for instance, with the Certificate and Diploma of the Chambers of Commerce and Industry in Paris and Lyon. The third type are courses based on case studies of actual business situations and transactions in the target country.

AUTONOMOUS IMPROVEMENT AND MAINTENANCE

How can I improve my knowledge of the language and culture if I cannot go abroad? If you are to become near-native in language use, you will need to refine your knowledge of the culture and pragmatics associated with the language you are trying to master. Where possible, you should seek out any native speakers in your community—exchange students or native-speaker aides, spouses or children of local business representatives, elderly residents who are first-generation immigrants and perhaps shut in or confined to rest homes, or children of short-term residents on special assignment. Involve yourself in host-family arrangements (whereby visiting speakers of the language are made to feel at home in the community), help with baby-sitting children, assist immigrants or visitors with formalities (like filling in applications, tax returns, or the like), or act as a tour guide to the local sights. On a college campus, seek out foreign students and help them learn to find their way about the campus and through the bureaucratic procedures; or offer to exchange an hour of English for an hour of conversation in their language.

Should it be impossible to make such contacts, then you will have to resort to vicarious help, through watching foreign-language films, in theaters, on television, or by renting them for your VCR, making it a point to observe ways of interacting, idiomatic turns of expression, turn-taking in discourse, gestures, exclamations, and fill-in expressions. In many areas there are ethnic sessions on the radio or even ethnic stations that broadcast in various languages throughout the day. Newscasts and commentaries can be accessed on shortwave radios from countries in which the language is spoken. Frequently one can hear songs in the other language, even on regular broadcasts. You should regularly read contemporary material, particularly novels and magazines that are read by students of your age in the target country. Correspond by letter or tape with a native speaker. If you do not have anyone to help you find such a correspondent, write a letter to the Chamber of Commerce, Tourist Information Office, or Head of the English Department in the high school of a town randomly selected, enclose a letter to an unknown correspondent introducing yourself, and ask the recipient to pass the letter on to a person of your age who would like to correspond with you. In all of these ways, you will develop a greater understanding of how native speakers of the target languages think and react. It depends on you to make the effort. Unfortunately, without such efforts we all decline rapidly from the peak of achievement we have attained in a language that is not our own.

WHAT ARE THE REALITIES?

What are the realities of finding a career in foreign languages? It is essential to emphasize at this point that knowledge of other languages alone will not ensure you a brilliant career, except as a teacher of languages, and even then you will need specialized training. Keep in mind that you must first and foremost be well qualified and competent in the specialized career area; it is for this that you will be employed. Unless language skill is part of the job specification, you may at first find that your language ability is underutilized and underappreciated, even when it seems to you that you have much more to contribute. Until you have more experience in your new career, you may need to create your own opportunities to use the language, and many have found that, with an employer or management unfamiliar with languages, they have had to propose programs and point out opportunities for which their knowledge of a language and culture made them uniquely useful.

Whether the fact is appreciated or not by U.S. executives, in business negotiations monolinguals can miss out on much of the peripheral discussion and often fail to recognize reactions that can make a difference to the outcome. They are left with what people choose to tell them. They cannot read the newspapers or trade reports that could alert them to trends and sensitivities. Furthermore, knowledge of the language and culture of one's counterparts is still needed for social contacts, in order to avoid making faux pas that may sour the atmosphere, and in order to interpret the behavior and responses of those with whom one is interacting.

The best method is probably to choose a career where a foreign language you know well could or ought to be considered useful. Then bide your time as you establish yourself in that career. Be ready to seize opportunities to incorporate that language in your work, looking ahead to the time when you will be able to make or influence decisions that determine the direction or development of your company, business, or agency.

ISN'T ENGLISH ENOUGH?

Isn't it a fact that English is becoming more and more the language of international business negotiations, conferences, and scientific and technical exchange of expertise? Doesn't this make knowledge of another language rather unimportant for the foreseeable future? The answer to these questions is yes and no. English is widely studied and used abroad, and most scientific research is either published in English or abstracted in English, but not all. (German, for instance, is now recognized as the language of engineering.) Yet many foreign nationals (perhaps most of them) prefer to conduct important negotiations in their native language, with the help of interpreters, so as not to be put at a disadvantage. In some countries, there is even a certain resentment of the advantages of the monolingual English speaker and a desire to force recognition of the value of the local language, the use of which is a matter of pride.

Smaller companies have less access to specialized services than large corporations, or cannot afford them, and, as a consequence, will eventually need more bilingual help as they try to contact small businesses abroad that are in the same situation. In service industries particularly, one is frequently interacting with less highly educated people who need linguistic help (as with court and hospital interpreters, World Health, relief and social service organizations).

In developing countries, the common language may well be Spanish, French, Arabic, or Swahili, rather than English. In Eastern Europe, German is in widespread use, partly because Germany produces important goods that these countries desperately need, and partly because of the historic and cultural ties. In fact, because of the economic strength of Germany, some predict that German may well become a *lingua franca* second only to English. The French, too, will certainly continue to see that their language is not pushed aside by their ancient rivals.

As a number of European countries come together in a union, there is still tension over what is viewed by some as the "linguistic imperialism" of English. These emotional reactions can be dissipated to some extent when the English-speaking negotiating or cooperating company or agency demonstrates a willingness to use other languages, recognizing the right of their partners to discuss important matters in the language with which they feel most comfortable. Transnational companies within Europe are well aware of these sensitivities; U.S.-based companies eventually will find that they must follow suit.

In summary, knowledge of another language will not necessarily help you get a position, unless it is part of the job specifications, but, along with cross-cultural experience, it may help you to perform your tasks more efficiently and successfully, thus leading to advancement. Prepare well for your career while keeping your language skills at a high level.

CHAPTER 2

IMPORTANCE OF FOREIGN LANGUAGES

At the end of World War II, the United States emerged as the richest and most powerful nation on earth. From a once geographically and culturally isolated nation, America today has assumed worldwide obligations. American commercial interests encompass the world. American cars run along the mountain roads of Greece; American music is played from Reykjavik to Rangoon; and American blue jeans can be obtained in remote hamlets of every continent.

It is significant that the United Nations, the body of international representatives working to establish peace and security, has its headquarters in America. At present, thousands of Americans are stationed abroad, and it is obvious that more will be called upon to serve their government abroad in the years to come. To meet these worldwide obligations and to maintain its cultural leadership, America must provide more effective training for its youth, particularly in foreign languages.

If America is to maintain its leadership in science, technology, industrial production, and world trade in today's rapidly evolving world, it cannot rest on its laurels, but must be able to compete with other multilingual contenders. There is and will continue to be an urgent demand for men and women who are in command of a foreign language. The need is apparent in seven major areas:

1. Industry and commerce: import-export, banking, finance, research, translation, interpreting
2. Scientific and professional use: engineering, research, law, medicine, library services, translation

3. United States government needs: overseas dependents' schools, overseas aid agencies, intelligence and law enforcement, the foreign service, translation, interpreting, broadcasting
4. United States armed forces: overseas duty, intelligence
5. Arts, media, and entertainment: foreign news coverage, book publishing, the performing arts, literary translation and research
6. Travel and tourism: travel services and related literature
7. Service: religious and volunteer agencies, teaching, international organizations, law enforcement, fire fighting, social work

THE WANT ADS

It is evident that there are many positions advertised every Sunday that require competence in a foreign language. The level of competence required in different jobs varies greatly. Sometimes it is quite moderate, as when, for instance, an ad reads: "Spanish would be useful" or "Knowledge of French helpful." On the other hand, there are many positions in which a higher degree of competence is required. The ad will then use specific terms such as: good knowledge, speak fluent, speak-write, speak-read, read-write, translation, dictation, or bilingual.

There is a wide range of occupations in which a foreign language, if not absolutely essential, still can be very useful. The Louisiana State Department of Education compiled the following list (here slightly adapted):

airline flight attendant	foreign exchange clerk
bilingual secretary	hotel manager
book dealer	immigration inspector
buyer	importer
Civil Service worker	intelligence officer
commercial attaché	international businessperson
consul	interpreter
customs inspector	journalist
diplomat	lawyer
exporter	librarian

philanthropist
physician
radio announcer
radio monitor
religious worker
receptionist
Red Cross volunteer
researcher
salesperson
social worker
trade magazine publisher

translator
teacher (exchange programs)
travel bureau worker
United Nations employee
U.S. government worker:
   armed services
   CIA
   Dept. of Defense
   Foreign Service
   U.S. Information Agency

As is evident from this list, the range is great. It goes all the way from the office clerk who did not complete high school but who speaks a foreign language, to the executive director of a huge corporation with offices in two dozen countries. Most of the positions, however, are clerical or secretarial.

Here are some typical want ads for persons with some knowledge of a foreign language:

SPANISH/ENGL SECY
Park Ave. co. Asst in translating Span
into Engl & vice/versa. Asst VP.

GERMAN/ENGLISH
Sec'y to Bank Executive
wd proc skills
Work bkgd reqd.

FRENCH-ENGLISH
Admin Assist.
Large prestige int'l corp for Sr
VP. Must have poise, tact, & be able
to deal with hi level mgmt.

BANKING INTERNATIONAL
Major West Coast Bank seeks int'l
deputy manager. Candidate must
have experience in Latin America.
Fluent Spanish, Title AVP or VP.

BILINGUAL CUSTOMER SERVICE
Spanish/English, type 40 wpm, general
office work. Permanent opportunity.

FRENCH SECY
Exec. Secy to President of new European
subsidiary.

CRUISE LINE/GERMAN
Exec. VP of large int'l corp. needs
secy with ad skills and admin.
abilities.

RUSSIAN TRANSLATORS
Engineers only.
Experienced in translating technical
specifications into Russian. Full
time, permanent.

It is evident, then, that there are many interesting positions waiting for
qualified persons with foreign language training combined with a technical skill. As we discussed in Chapter 1, knowledge of a foreign language alone will not secure the job, but it is an important and, in some
cases, an essential asset.

COMMENTS OF BUSINESS AND PROFESSIONAL PEOPLE

Dr. John H. Furbay, former Director of Air World Education, Kansas
City, Missouri, said in his bulletin, *Global Minds for an Air World:*

We are going to have to get used to neighbors not only with ... different
religions, but neighbors speaking different languages. We are a one-

language country. American travelers are embarrassed on finding that so many other peoples speak several languages. We are probably the only major country in the world whose educated class speaks only one language—their mother tongue. This is a real problem for airlines and other business firms who are trying to staff their offices in several countries. Where are they going to find American employees who can speak several languages? A business representative can't say to a prospective customer. "If you only knew English, I have something good I could sell you." We must learn other languages if we are going to have a place of leadership in the world, either commercial or political.

A similar thought was expressed by Alex J. Wertis, who at the time was Personnel Director of the United States Steel Export Company:

> The ability to speak or to learn a foreign language is a tremendous asset. The greatest criticism of Americans in foreign lands in the past has been their reluctance to meet other peoples half-way about language. Other peoples take as much pride in their language and culture as we do in ours. To address them in their own speech is a compliment to their language and culture. It gives you a head start in personal relations. I do not have to tell you about the success that the army and navy have had in teaching languages, even English.

George Bain, principal of the London Business School, writes:

> Americans who spend time studying or working abroad realize that they're the ones speaking English with an accent . . . (in business). If you're buying, you can get away with operating in your own tongue. If you're selling, it certainly helps to speak the customer's language.

H. W. Burch of the United Press Association, New York, summarizing the need of a foreign language equipment for world journalism, wrote:

> There are, in fact, so many visible opportunities for the bilingual or trilingual person that no persuasion should be needed for the aspiring student or adult to perfect [himself or herself] in a foreign language.

L. B. Morgan, then Manager Export Sales, Colorado Fuel & Iron Corporation, New York, stressed the importance of Spanish:

> There is indeed a vital need in export organizations for young people with a knowledge of a foreign language. Because of the preponderance of

trade with Latin America in our export department, a thorough knowledge of Spanish in all its phases is absolutely *de rigueur.* Apart from the practical consideration of this question affecting individual organizations in the conduct of their business, there is the cultural factor that, in the mounting interest in international affairs, should receive greater emphasis. It is obvious that a knowledge of languages fosters good will and understanding, which in the long run will redound to our national interest.

It must be stressed, however, that the majority of business positions require a technical knowledge within a given field. Even interpreters and translators need knowledge of technical operations to be able to transpose meaning accurately. The manager of the Industrial Relations Department of the International Harvester Co. wrote:

> ... the knowledge of a foreign language is an asset, but of minor consideration as it must be used in conjunction with a specialized trade or profession, such as documentation clerk, bilingual stenographer, diplomatic clerk, etc. These latter functions set the salary more so than the knowledge of a foreign language. When we at Harvester are considering a person for foreign service, the fact that [he or she] can speak a foreign language is considered only when all other requirements have been met. This means a clear understanding of Harvester management and sales policies and expertness in a particular line, such as manufacturing, engineering, and knowledge of the functions of our products.

Esther Newman of the Pan American Broadcasting Company wrote:

> From time to time, we do require the services of individuals with reading and writing capabilities in French, Spanish, and German in both our secretarial and bookkeeping departments. I would recommend, based on our experience, that business usage should be included in the foreign language curriculum in the schools. We have found that, given the best training in the world and with the utmost competence on the part of the student, without a grounding in the business usage of the language involved—particularly financial—students are inadequately prepared to use their foreign language knowledge in the business world.

Charles C. Mentzer, Manager of Personnel, International General Electric Company, wrote:

> The International General Electric Company has representation in practically every country of the free world ... With this wide range of

contact, we have certain positions where competence in a foreign language by employees is absolutely essential in order to perform the work required. . . .

Probably the most prevalent language for our purposes is Spanish. Portuguese, French, and German are being required more often . . . employees must first have technical competence to perform the work, thus the knowledge of a language is placed second or third in importance in our selection process. . . . In a number of positions, our secretaries are required to take dictation in a foreign language. . . . In field positions, such as sales, product service, engineering, application engineering, and manufacturing, the ability for a person to converse in the required language is most important. . . .

Stephen A. Schoff, Vice President, Personnel, Pepsi-Cola International, wrote:

Insofar as our overseas operations are concerned, bilingual ability is almost a prerequisite other than in areas where English is the predominant language, i.e., Australia or parts of Africa. Anyone assigned abroad to any other area definitely would need Spanish, French, German, or Urdu, as the case might be. We generally look for a prospective employee who has a college education, marketing background, and some previous industry experience, in addition to a language ability.

Robert L. Michelson, while Assistant to the Vice President of Honeywell, Inc., expressed similar thoughts. This company has plants in Canada, Scotland, and Holland and subsidiaries in Sweden, Belgium, Switzerland, France, Mexico, and Puerto Rico.

The ability to speak and write a foreign language is indeed an asset but is not a necessity for someone who works in international operations in the United States. However, if that person is transferred to a foreign country to head up one of our subsidiaries, for example, then it becomes important that [he or she] learn to communicate fluently in the language of that country.

The last statement is, of course, very encouraging to those with language competence.

SALARIES

The salaries paid to persons who use a foreign language vocationally depends, of course, on the degree of skill and the technical knowledge involved. Competence in a language may range all the way from that of a librarian who can identify titles of books in three or four languages, to that of an editor who writes technical articles in French or Spanish; from that of the interpreter who is required to ask only a set of simple, standardized questions, to that of the UN expert who has to turn outbursts of emotionally high-strung foreign delegates into correct, idiomatic English. For the ordinary business job it may be said that the average office worker earns more per week because of a knowledge of a foreign language than a co-worker in a comparable position who is not required to know a foreign language.

Emilio Mayer, who was a leading official of the Banca Commerciale Italiana, said:

> Personnel with a thorough knowledge of foreign languages are generally much better paid. They occupy key positions and, inasmuch as they are hard to replace, they are usually the last ones to be dismissed in the event of a reduction in personnel.

In short, then, it may be said that, because knowledge of a foreign language is an added asset, it will be reflected in additional compensation, comparatively modest in the case of the office workers, and considerable in the case of the highly responsible executive. It all depends on the training and experience of the applicant.

PERSONAL ATTRIBUTES FOR SUCCESS

One of the primary phases of language learning is the acquisition and retention of a large stock of words and idioms; hence, the importance of memory. But even the possession of an extensive vocabulary does not make one a speaker or writer in the foreign tongue. The words must be combined correctly in sentences and thought groups for specific situations; hence, the importance of imagination.

Since oral expression is necessarily rapid, the mental processes must be almost instantaneous; the quick thinker is also the more effective speaker and writer. Learning the printed language is helped by a sense of logical sequence and analogy. Learning the spoken tongue is greatly facilitated by imitativeness. Children learn to speak almost exclusively by means of this ability. Persons who possess this gift can repeat correctly entire sentences even in a difficult foreign tongue, despite the fact that they do not know their meaning. Finally, there must be built up, through constant practice, a sense of what is correct and incorrect. It becomes almost instinctive; it is known scientifically as *sprachgefühl,* or a "feeling for language."

In addition to the mental functions mentioned above, there are also several physical ones. For speaking, the most important one is flexibility and adaptiveness of the vocal organs. Children usually learn to speak a language with ease because movement of their teeth, tongue, and vocal cords is not yet habitual. Adults often experience greater difficulty in speaking a new tongue for this reason and also because for years they have employed only certain mouth formations. In this connection, phonetics, which aims to describe sounds and their correct production, is helpful. However, the younger person still has a considerable advantage in learning to speak a foreign language.

Different people possess linguistic facility in varying degrees. George Bernard Shaw knew several European languages, but he did not speak them well, although he was a genius in English. On the other hand, many waiters can converse glibly in five or six languages.

A native-born American with some degree of mastery of the foreign language will have more opportunities in the business world. Of course, ambitious and conscientious persons, once they have jobs, will make every effort to improve their command of the foreign language and thus prepare themselves for higher positions.

CHAPTER 3

EDUCATIONAL TRAINING

Beginning with secondary education, students should prepare for training in a foreign language. Because in many cases the vocational use of a foreign language is combined with some other technical activity—such as international trade or engineering—it is wise to adjust one's educational preparation accordingly. If one plans a career that requires a high degree of technical ability, one will need to continue training at a college and possibly at a professional school. As in all fields, the principle will hold true that the longer the training, the greater the skill; the greater the skill, the higher the salary.

SECONDARY SCHOOL

In most metropolitan areas throughout the United States, high schools offer the standard languages—French, German, Spanish, and Italian. In addition, because of local conditions and the presence of various nationalities, other languages also may appear in the high school curriculum. Among these are Italian, Portuguese, Hebrew, Norwegian, Hungarian, Polish, and Russian. Because of a changing world situation, Japanese and Chinese courses are becoming more common.

Most high schools offer three years of a foreign language, with a fourth year usually dedicated to advanced placement. Many junior high schools now offer language instruction. Also, there are now throughout the country many cities in which a foreign language, generally Spanish or French, is taught in the early elementary grades. An increasing number of schools are introducing not only programs where a second language is taught, but also so-called immersion classes, in which one or more subjects are taught entirely in a foreign language.

It is important for the future linguist to begin language studies as early as possible. There is nothing more valuable than a firm grounding in the language at an early age. There may be some difficulty, especially in smaller communities, in pursuing certain languages. Fortunately, however, the language most in demand in business is also the most widely taught throughout the country—namely Spanish.

If at all feasible, the young linguist should begin a second language after a year or two of a first one. In order to make good progress, the student should not only do the regular school assignments, but also take advantage of every opportunity to get practice in the foreign language, especially in speaking.

COLLEGE

Learning another language takes time. On the average, three years of study in secondary school is an absolute necessity. Since college preparation would be necessary for management and technical positions, every effort should be made to continue with language instruction at that level. Many higher institutions permit incoming students to exempt courses by examination. In this way students can take courses that will provide them with an even greater variety. It would be wise to spread out language study so that upon graduation the language capability has not atrophied from lack of practice just at the time it is needed most. A student intending to use the language as a career skill should continue with advanced-level courses in that language, since a thorough knowledge of one foreign language will be more valuable than a smattering of two different ones.

CHOICE OF A FOREIGN LANGUAGE

Which language to pursue in high school depends largely on the field of work one is planning to enter. For export trade with Latin America it would undoubtedly be Spanish, although the addition of Portuguese would be useful later for the Brazilian market. Frequently, a young person does not know precisely what profession he or she will enter. In such a case, it is justifiable to follow personal preference or to choose according to college requirements. In addition, educational and vocational guidance can be helpful to students in making wise career choices.

In a pamphlet entitled *What Foreign Languages Shall I Study During Secondary School?* Roland B. Greeley, Director of Admissions at the Massachusetts Institute of Technology, made the following interesting and useful recommendations:

> The knowledge of foreign languages is always desirable and frequently essential for the future scientist and engineer. Study should begin as early as possible, with the choice of languages dependent on factors which vary according to the individual. . . .
>
> The study of a foreign language, ancient or modern, broadens the student's cultural and intellectual horizon. In addition to its value in the enrichment of mind and culture, the study of language has practical uses. It furthers commercial, scientific, and social intercourse with foreign countries. Facility in colloquial speech is likely to be of particular value in this kind of work. The United States is developing closer contacts with the rest of the world than ever before. It follows that leaders in every field will increasingly need to be conversant with foreign conditions and foreign tongues. Foreign languages are a necessary part of the training of those who aspire to responsible leadership. American engineers, scientists, architects, and executives are likely to have increasing need for oral language proficiency in order to compete with professionals of other countries, who have a long tradition of language facility.
>
> Another practical reason for language study concerns the specialized purposes of research. It is true that many practicing engineers in this country—for example, those concerned with construction, industrial production, management, accounting or domestic marketing as these activities relate to technology—have little or no professional need for a foreign language. On the other hand, those whose work involves research or design problems of a fundamental nature need to be in constant touch with developments in other countries. Most scientific and technical reports, periodicals, and other documents, including patents, are not available in translation. It follows that at least a reading knowledge of several foreign languages is important for the research scientist or engineer.

The study of foreign languages should, in general, commence as early in life as possible. There is no quick and easy answer to the question "What language should I study?" The answer must take into account the individual student's tastes and interests, the educational opportunities available, and the probable future field of work. Perhaps the most helpful approach to the question will be a brief discussion of the languages that are likely to be important to a future scientist or engineer.

Spanish. This language is spoken in more homes in the United States than any other except English. Since many non-Spanish speaking Americans have regular social and business contacts with this large minority, it is a natural first choice of many language students, especially in Florida and in the Southwestern United States. Our increasing import and export trade with Latin America and the Caribbean is an important reason for considering Spanish. Social workers, health professionals, police officers, and firefighters have increasing need for Spanish in urban areas. Students of Spanish would be well advised to add Portuguese to their repertoire of languages at a later date.

German. There is in German a considerable backlog of scientific literature to which access is important for the research worker. Many scientific reports from the countries of Central Europe and Scandinavia have been published in German. The language therefore has a scientific significance that goes beyond the cultural contributions of Germany itself. Our extensive trade with Germany provides another major reason for considering German. With the rapid changes in Eastern Europe, German is gaining in importance, and Germany as a strong economic power has considerable influence in the new Europe. In engineering, knowledge of German is particularly important.

French. In general, the French are at their best in treating the sciences in their pure or theoretical aspects. In many of these areas, French thought is preeminent. There exists in French an important scientific literature, particularly in biology, mathematics, physics, and chemistry. French is still a major language of communication in international affairs and is widely used in certain Arabic countries, in large areas of Africa, and some parts of the Caribbean. It is of major importance in literature and film studies.

Russian. The former Soviet Union had become a leader in scientific research. In such fields as aerodynamics, electronics, mathematics, metallurgy, nuclear science and engineering, and theoretical physics, Russian publications have been significant. Inability to keep abreast of Russian developments has been a severe handicap. America needs many more people trained in reading technical Russian, in addition to competent speakers of that language for purposes of trade as new markets open up.

Japanese. With the emergence of Japan as a strong economic power and a political force in world affairs, Japanese has become the most rapidly growing language for study in American schools and colleges. Ability to communicate in Japanese requires insight into a very different culture. Learning to read Japanese is a lengthy process because of the use of two syllabaries (Hiragana for Japanese words, Katakana for foreign words) and thousands of Chinese characters (Kanji). Competence in Japanese is a highly appreciated asset for international business.

Chinese. This language is spoken by the more than one billion inhabitants on the Chinese mainland and also in important business centers like Taiwan, Singapore, and Hong Kong. A tone language with very different structure from English, Chinese uses thousands of characters that must be mastered in order to be able to read the language. It is, however, fascinating to study, and enrollments are on the rise in American educational institutions. Competence in Chinese is definitely a career asset for international business.

Italian. A growing number of students, often for ethnic or religious reasons, are studying Italian. Within the new Europe, Italy has a substantial place as a commercial and manufacturing partner. Italian, like German, is also of interest to students of music, particularly opera; it also attracts those interested in archaeology, art, and architecture.

Hebrew. Hebrew is essential for certain areas of archaeological research, as well as for biblical research, and for students who wish to study or work in Israel.

Arabic. Arabic is an extremely important world language and is mostly taught in colleges. Unfortunately, opportunities for careers in Arabic are not plentiful outside of government agencies.

Key Languages. Looking ahead to the probable future complexion of the world, it appears that Arabic, Italian, and Portuguese will assume much greater importance for Americans.

YOUR DECISION

There is little doubt that adding a foreign language component to your engineering, economics, chemistry, or physics major can give that extra selling point needed to secure employment. Beyond this, it can be a key to advancement on the job. It also can be an important factor when travel or overseas employment are being considered. Notice the choice of the word *can.* It is not the intention of this book to depict foreign language acquisition as a panacea in one's search for a career. Indeed most jobs in the United States do not require any knowledge of a foreign language at all. Some people find learning another language difficult and would rather pursue other interests. On the other hand, growing numbers of students are having a pleasant introduction to another culture and its language through classes in the elementary schools. Others have begun a foreign language in high school or college just to fill a requirement, but they have experienced success in it and have begun to enjoy the satisfaction of their increasing command of it. Still others have come to realize the value of speaking another language through travel or simply through an awareness of the increasingly international nature of business, government, communications, science, entertainment, and tourism.

The question then that arises is "Where can I best make use of a foreign language?" There are three categories of need for a foreign language:

1. Language as a primary skill—essential to get job
2. Language as an auxiliary skill—highly useful or required
3. Language as an auxiliary skill—useful with other skills

Without doubt, the career requiring the most intensive language study is that of a simultaneous translator, whereby the spoken word must be interpreted in another language. Such translation must be made immediately, often involving a wide variety of topics in the midst of heated debate such as at the UN or other international bodies. Training for such rigorous work is available only at a limited number of institutions of higher learning. It is clear that such a career will be limited to a relatively small group of linguists, most of whom have bilingual or trilingual advantages. Most language students will need to look elsewhere for a career in which they can make use of their linguistic abilities.

At this point one would need to ask questions such as "Am I interested in teaching a foreign language?" "Am I particularly good at translating the written word into English?" "Could I make use of my foreign language with a multinational corporation?" "Am I interested in governmental service overseas?" "Would travel and tourism provide me with a fulfilling life?" "Can I make use of a foreign language in a scientific or professional career?" Obviously many questions could be asked. It is not within the scope of this book to make recommendations concerning your other major areas of interest. Many volumes have been written on this topic. All schools and colleges have counselors and publications available. The United States Department of Labor publishes the *Occupational Outlook Handbook,* which tells what various jobs are like, how to qualify and train for them, and where they are located. This large volume is revised every two years.

Another step in your search is to obtain more specific information concerning your future plans, which are perhaps now for the first time coming into focus. If you are interested in government service, you might write to one or more governmental agencies that need linguists (see Chapter 6 for information). Or if you are considering employment with a multinational corporation, locate the *Directory of American Firms Operating in Foreign Countries* (13th edition, 1994). Here you can find the locations of the overseas branches of some 2,600 American companies. In addition, 127 countries from Afghanistan to Zimbabwe are listed alphabetically, with 19,000 American subsidiaries noted. If your library does not have the most current edition, a brochure supplied by the Chamber of Commerce of the United States can provide you with the addresses of all foreign offices of the chamber (see Appendix B). From such offices specific information concerning American business in a given country frequently can be obtained. Each individual state development board can undoubtedly provide you with a list of corporations that are involved locally in international commerce. A visit to some of these companies in your area might be very helpful to see how a language could fit into the employment picture. Not to be forgotten either are the numerous foreign firms with American affiliates. They generally give greater consideration to a person with the technical skills they need who also has foreign language facility.

One of your sources of reference may be the *Encyclopedia of Associations,* which lists 23,000 national, international, business, trade, fraternal, ethnic, and other clubs and organizations along with their mailing addresses, officers, total membership, and statement of purpose. A librarian also would be able to help you find other sources of addresses and information. Obviously, the more you know about the foreign language requirements or the possibilities for language use in a given position, the better you will be able to prepare yourself by selecting the most appropriate types of language courses. If conversational ability is likely to be needed, then conversation courses should be taken. If mainly translation skills will be required, appropriate courses on translation techniques would be absolutely essential. Regardless of which type of linguistic skills you will be called upon to use, an understanding of the culture and customs of the target language speakers is indispensable, especially if you would like to work in that country. Most colleges offer such courses, in association with language study.

GETTING PRACTICE

Learning a language thoroughly requires time, patience, and practice. It cannot be done solely in school; with the large classes the opportunity for practice consists of but a few minutes daily for the individual student. It is as with the learning of the piano; it is not the one lesson a week that counts in the acquisition of dexterity, but the hours of practice before and after the lesson.

In the case of language learning particularly, basic structure and vocabulary must be so well internalized that the speaker can concentrate on expressing nuances of meaning through the language.

The earnest language student will try to do some additional reading. A pleasant way to develop confident reading without constantly running to a dictionary is to regularly read foreign language magazines and newspapers in the language. These are a fruitful source of up-to-date vocabulary and idioms for the more advanced student. Some should be available in your school or college library; if they are not, ask your instructor to order some. Newspapers from abroad can be subscribed to or obtained from certain newsdealers. In most metropolitan areas, dailies and weeklies are published in foreign languages. In New York, for instance, there are such in French, German, Italian, Spanish, Portuguese, Russian, Polish, Norwegian, Arabic, Yiddish, Greek, and Czech.

There are a number of excellent magazines published in foreign languages. There is the universally known *Reader's Digest,* which comes in nineteen different languages. Since it contains articles on every conceivable subject, it is a gold mine for technical expressions, idioms, and new colloquialisms. It is helpful to record these in a notebook and try to use them.

Light reading also helps you to guess the meaning of new words from context or ignore those that are not essential to the overall meaning. Short contemporary novels, detective stories, or science fiction are entertaining and useful. Ask your teacher to recommend some easy but interesting books of this type, or search the library for some. Books of short stories and contemporary plays may be a good way to begin.

Listening to the spoken language is excellent practice. This can be done conveniently with the radio, cassettes, or compact discs. In many metropolitan areas, there are a number of stations that broadcast programs in foreign languages. In New York, for example, Italian, Yiddish, German, Polish, Russian, and Spanish may be heard daily.

There are several companies that specialize in foreign language recordings. Recordings of popular singers are readily available, and films in the foreign language may be viewed on television, in local theaters, or rented for your VCR. (Make sure you rent one with the original foreign language soundtrack.) There are also recordings of poetry, and dramatic and literary selections spoken by experts or well-known actors. These provide excellent models for pronunciation and intonation.

Radios with short wave capability have become relatively inexpensive. Short-wave programs in countless foreign languages are available twenty-four hours a day. A letter to the appropriate embassy or cultural agency would enable you to obtain free broadcast schedules.

Anyone who is really serious about learning another language should consider the possibility of traveling to the country or countries where the target language is spoken. Reduced rates for students and special package tours are good incentives for people who want to see the world outside the United States. While such a trip would certainly be beneficial, far more value can be derived from an overseas experience by organized study-abroad or international exchange programs. Studying the language for credit in the environment where the language is heard and seen at every turn greatly speeds the learning process. International programs that include arrangements for living with a family add an even greater dimension and invaluable insights into the real culture of the country. Two such programs are the Experiment in International Living and the German-American Partnership Program (GAPP). There are many others sponsored by educational institutions. Always check with your instructor to ensure that the program is a respectable one.

For those who desire a real "feather in their cap" to be included in their resumes, probably the epitome would be a year abroad as a Fulbright exchange student at a foreign university or a year with the International Student Exchange Program (ISEP). Admittedly only the best students will be found among their ranks.

Some simply cannot afford the cost of the programs mentioned above. However, they may be able to secure a summer job in the country of their choice in one of the popular American fast-food restaurants found in many cities outside the United States. There are numerous camps for Americans throughout the world where American young people can find employment. Some agencies such as the Council on International Educational Exchange (CIEE) arrange work in various countries for a modest fee. Often overlooked in this country are the opportunities offered by the numerous "international work camps" scattered throughout the world. In return for work on public and community projects, participants receive room and board. For some, the contact with people from various cultures and the opportunity to travel on weekends make up for the lack of financial remuneration.

If the likelihood of a trip to another country seems remote, a good substitute is to obtain a pen pal through a letter exchange agency. Very frequently language teachers or professors can provide contacts for pen pals in the country whose language they are teaching. Should a trip become a reality, the excitement of spending time in the home of a pen pal is an experience that will not be forgotten. Such letter or tape exchanges can serve a number of purposes, not the least of which is making the participants aware of the differences as well as the similarities between their respective countries.

SPECIAL TRAINING

A high school course of three or four years in a language, together with the business training given in the commercial department, will suffice for an office job. However, college training is advisable for higher positions in business and civil service and is indispensable for teaching and scholarly research. In addition, for the person hoping to become a highly paid executive with a near-native command of a language, there are the Berlitz Schools. They are known all over the world and teach every spoken language. There are more than 60 schools in the United States and more than 200 schools in twenty-three countries on five continents.

Another special school is the Latin American Institute, which prepares students primarily for positions requiring Spanish, Portuguese, or French. The Institute will, however, offer German or Russian if there is a sufficient demand. Excellent courses are provided in secretarial work, diplomatic and foreign service, and foreign trade. These courses usually require two years to complete.

One of the best language schools is the School of Languages and Linguistics in Washington, DC, which is part of the School of Foreign Service of Georgetown University. The school is "dedicated to the preparation of men and women for diplomatic and consular service, foreign trade, international shipping, business careers, overseas activities, and public administration." It is "designed to offer specialized instruction to selected candidates whose actual or contemplated professional activities require an effective knowledge of languages." The school also does research in applied linguistics and in the field of language methodology. Correlated courses in geography, history, civilization, and contemporary problems are conducted in several major languages, as well as courses in foreign relations, international law, and world economics.

With its elaborate electronic equipment, the school provides opportunity for training in translation and interpreting. The languages students can major in are French, German, Spanish, Portuguese, Arabic, Italian, Japanese, Russian, and Chinese. The school is continually expanding its facilities.

There are numerous summer language schools for teachers. Those maintained abroad by some of the universities and colleges are highly recommended. For example, New York University has summer institutes in Europe and offers an internship program for students to apply their language skills to "the outside world." In three summer sessions a student can acquire enough credits for the master's degree.

In every large city there are language schools, like those of Berlitz, where instruction is given by natives. Of course, the finishing touch of the language student's training is a trip abroad with an extended stay in the country whose language is her or his specialty.

BILINGUAL OFFICE JOB TRAINING

As was stated before, a good high school course in a foreign language and commercial subjects will prepare you for an office job. If, however, you are ambitious and want a more attractive position with a better paying salary, it is advisable to take some courses at a recognized business school. In fact, the average business owner or operator usually prefers the graduate of a private business college to the product of a public high school.

There are, of course, different kinds of positions on various levels and different kinds of training programs. The Latin American Institute trains high school graduates for business, offering the following programs:

private secretary
bilingual secretary
diplomatic and executive secretary
foreign trade secretary
translator and interpreter
export-import traffic manager
intensive courses for college graduates

PLANNING YOUR COURSES

Since in most cases the vocational use of a foreign language is combined with some other technical skill—such as secretarial work, international trade, engineering, or marketing—it is wise to plan one's educational preparation accordingly. Beginning with secondary education, provision should be made for training in a foreign language and in other major academic subjects. In preparation for a career that requires a high degree of technical skill, advanced courses at a university or professional institute are highly recommended. As in all fields, the principle will hold true that the longer the training, the greater the skill; the greater the skill, the higher the salary.

Studies have been made of the incidence of various college majors in combination with foreign language skill. Ranked in order of frequency, in a recent study, they included: business administration and management, marketing and sales, engineering, secretarial skills, finance, international relations, accounting, economics, clerical skills, communications, law, public relations, advertising, data processing, English language skills, civil engineering, journalism, statistics, psychology, library skills, cultural studies, public administration, sociology, political science, and fine arts.

Many major corporations also incorporate foreign language in their training programs or hire individuals who have combinations of skills like those listed above. Some of the largest of these corporations are Exxon, General Motors, Ford Motor Co., Texaco, Mobil, Standard Oil, Gulf Oil, IBM, General Electric, Chrysler, Shell Oil, Atlantic Richfield, Du Pont (I.E.) de Nemours, Continental Oil, Western Electric, Procter & Gamble, Tenneco, Union Carbide, Westinghouse Electric, Goodyear Tire & Rubber, and Phillips Petroleum.

GOVERNMENT SERVICE

In preparing for the Foreign Service, you should broaden your courses to include geography, economics, money and banking, diplomatic correspondence, and international law.

Preparation for the position of Foreign Service Officer should include, in addition to foreign languages, American history and government, international diplomatic protocol, economic and political geography, and consular documents.

Special secretarial training will qualify you for the following jobs: diplomatic secretary, consular assistant, executive secretary, translator, interpreter, or bilingual secretary.

The following courses are recommended for the future Foreign Service officer:

American history	international law
American government	economic and political
diplomatic history	geography
Latin American history	business English
European history	diplomatic correspondence
international relations	economics
money and banking	grammar
English stenography	conversation
typing	composition
word processing and computing	commercial correspondence
foreign language	translation technique

INTERNATIONAL CAREERS

More and more university students are giving thought to the idea of training for a career involving a multinational corporation. A number of graduate programs throughout the country can point to some impressive statistics concerning percentage of placement of graduates as well as excellent starting salaries. In most programs, foreign language acquisition or English for foreign students is a major component of the program. For example, the brochure for the *Masters of International Business Studies (MIBS)* at the University of South Carolina has the following to say about the reasons behind its program:

> The tremendous growth of international business has evoked a corresponding need for internationally trained and skilled business executives. In turn, schools of business have attempted to respond to this demand by revising their curricula to include international topics and courses. Rather than engage in patchwork or cosmetic changes in existing curricula, the

University of South Carolina decided to develop a new business degree program which would meet more specifically the needs of multinational corporations. The MIBS program is founded on these basic principles:

- The successful international manager must have a real graduate business degree. The course of study must include both fundamental topics and advanced work in areas of concern to multinational enterprises.
- The international business executive must have the ability to communicate in at least one language other than her or his own, and must have the ability to learn additional languages quickly, as needed.
- The international business executive must be attuned to the cultural differences which exist around the world and their impact on how business is done.

The MIBS degree program incorporates each of these objectives in a program of study lasting two years:

- Students develop skills in a foreign language through an Accelerated Language Training Course.
- An Area Studies segment provides students with the opportunity to develop their acculturation skills.
- A completely Internationalized Business Curriculum provides both the fundamental marketing, operations management, export-import techniques, and more. These segments are coordinated and scheduled interdependently, so as to enhance your perception of their interrelationships and to utilize your time most efficiently. This truly comprehensive curriculum provides the necessary skills for your internship assignment and the basics for more advanced specialized work.

Language and cultural training are carried out at the main campus as well as at various overseas sites. By the conclusion of the on-site training, students should be ready for their six-month internships with a multinational corporation. At present, six languages are offered: French, German, Spanish, Portuguese, Arabic, and Japanese.

The Academy of International Business ranks the top international business graduate schools as follows: New York University, University of South Carolina, University of Pennsylvania, Columbia University, and Harvard University.

At the undergraduate level you should look into the possibility of majoring in a foreign language and minoring in accounting or business administration. Possibly a double major with another department would be best. In such cases, a talk with an advisor in the language department should be helpful.

A growing number of institutions are providing undergraduate language students some very exciting opportunities for making use of not only their language capabilities but also their knowledge in another field. This concept, that of the international cooperative program, was developed into its most workable form at Michigan State University. After students have had sufficient language and business or other training, they are then assigned to a job with a multinational company, ideally working in a plant overseas. The program has grown by leaps and bounds, so that now a number of colleges and universities are associated with Michigan State in a consortium arrangement to provide a wider selection of opportunities. Some universities also provide special courses of study for government service abroad.

CHAPTER 4

THE JOB SEARCH

While one generally thinks of the job-finding aspect of college or high school training as one of the last steps, in reality the process should begin long before graduation. As soon as some of the basic questions mentioned in a previous chapter have been answered, the student should make gradual but regular efforts to obtain as much information as possible. The advice of family and friends should be sought first. Not everyone, of course, will have "connections," but it certainly is a legitimate way to gain at least initial contact with a company or organization.

The vocational guidance office at your school or college will have a well-stocked library of books and pamphlets. The counselors are there to help you, and they have a wealth of experience you can draw upon. Companies make arrangements for interviewing potential employees through such offices. Short courses or seminars are frequently offered by the guidance office on the various aspects of the job search. Individual counseling is also available. Some guidance offices make arrangements with alumni of the school who have indicated a willingness to talk with interested students at their place of business. Such conversations with concerned alumni can be very helpful in answering many questions. The counselors also can recommend reading materials. There is no shortage of books that deal with the very practical aspects of getting a job, such as writing a letter of application, going to a job interview, following up, and analyzing possible job alternatives (see Appendix D for additional job search materials).

As we have already seen, the daily newspaper is a fruitful source of want ads for jobs requiring a foreign language. Admittedly, one finds a greater number of such opportunities in the larger metropolitan areas.

LETTER OF APPLICATION

The letter applying for a position should be composed and written with great care, for your application may compete with hundreds of others. Each will be judged by its appearance, correctness of English, ease of style, and contents. The following are a few helpful suggestions:

- If possible, address an individual in the firm, using the person's full name and correct title.
- Instead of implying that you are looking for a job, offer your services.
- Indicate that you know what the job is about and that you are genuinely interested.
- Show that your previous experience has prepared you for the job.
- Be specific about your qualifications and the results you have obtained in the past.
- Make your letter stand out by using personal description; avoid anything stereotyped.
- Try to have an effective opening sentence and a strong closing sentence.
- Avoid hackneyed or stereotyped phrases; write naturally and sincerely, but be modest in expressing opinions.
- Check your letter for errors in grammar, spelling, and punctuation.
- Remember, "Brevity is the soul of wit." Delete unnecessary words and phrases; do not repeat yourself.
- Mention two or three references. In addition to their addresses, give their job titles and telephone numbers, if possible.
- If you have a good letter of reference, you might photocopy it and enclose a copy in your letter of application.

PERSONAL INTERVIEW

If you are called for a personal interview, your aim, of course, will be to make as good an impression as possible. The two major factors in any application for a job are *competence* and *personality.* The former is largely a matter of training and intelligence and reveals itself best on the job. Even if the personnel manager should go to the trouble of giving you a test, all your potential skills will not be discovered.

In applying for a position, you are judged primarily on the basis of personality. This consists of a combination of such factors as appearance including neatness and grooming, poise, manners, and speech.

The personal traits generally rated highest in a candidate are intelligence, accuracy, good judgment, efficiency, loyalty, adaptiveness, and executive ability. The employer may ask questions to determine whether you possess some of the above qualities.

In addition to your other qualifications, make a special point to emphasize the extent of your language background. Be certain to mention specialized courses you might have taken, such as "Business French" or "Scientific German." Also important is any study abroad experience that would indicate a greater understanding of the culture. Your language skills may be just the extra something that gets you a job offer.

EMPLOYMENT AGENCIES

There are a great number of employment agencies, especially in large cities, but only a few of them specialize in jobs with foreign language requirements. The agency, of course, charges a fee for securing the job for the applicant. In many cases, however, the employer will take care of this expense, and often this fact is stated in the want ad.

In addition to commercial agencies, there are various government offices through which employment may be obtained, including the state employment services. Federal employment is taken care of by the Civil Service Commission, which maintains offices in principal cities.

EMPLOYMENT ABROAD

When you seek a position in the export field, you will probably be asked if you will work in the home office or in a foreign country. Some firms prepare their young employees or, at least, a limited number of them, for service in Latin America. A knowledge of Spanish is, of course, of great importance. We must not, however, forget Brazil, one of the largest buyers of American goods in South America, whose language is Portuguese. Some of the large U.S. companies doing business in that country are: General Electric, Ford Motor Company, Exxon, Sears,

Union Carbide, and NCR. A major portion of the executives and technical experts of these companies are Americans.

It is interesting to note what qualifications are required in connection with higher positions in the export field and what jobs are available. The following advertisement was taken from *The Exporter,* a trade journal:

Far Eastern Representative

Leading manufacturer of well known industrial products seeks sales representative for Far East. Substantial opportunity exists for person with capabilities to eventually assume complete responsibility for sales, licensing, and investment program now under way in the area. This is a career position involving indefinite foreign residence and considerable travel. Applicants must have work experience in foreign trade, mature judgment, and ability to plan own work program and carry it out effectively without constant direction from headquarters. Submit complete resume, salary requirements, and letter stating why you qualify for this position.

Some people, however, obtain positions by advertising themselves. Here are two such advertisements:

Export Sales Manager

Will help to establish or increase your export sales. Top experience export marketing and manufacturing. Intimate knowledge Latin American (18 years' residence) and European markets. Fluent Spanish, German, French, and others. Willing part-time travel from New York City base. European college degree. Seeks challenging export sales position.

Foreign Consultant, Associate

Aggressive American executive with Swiss background and training, 30 years' experience in foreign business, international trade, and establishing organizations overseas, available as consultant or full-time associate. Speaks several languages fluently. Wide administrative and sales experience in Far East, Europe, Canada, Africa, and U.S.A.

Securing a Job in South America

For those interested in obtaining a position in a South American country, the following information will be valuable. It is taken from a report prepared by J. Silvado Bueno of the Foreign Trade Office, Pan American Union, Washington, DC:

United States citizens who wish to work in Latin America are advised to seek employment with North American firms. Some outstanding reasons for this follow:

(a) the guarantee of work, before departing from the United States, provided by a contract with such a firm.

(b) the advantage of salary payment, usually in dollars, or half in dollars and half in the currency of the country in which one is to work.

(c) the 'cost of living allowance' where living costs are highly inflated. (This seems to be a general policy among United States companies.)

(d) the possibility that the candidate for work has not had an opportunity to become proficient in Spanish, Portuguese, or French, and this deficiency may not constitute an insurmountable barrier when he is employed by a North American concern.

Attention is called to the fact that openings in Latin America are generally limited in scope and number. While there are some opportunities for those trained in bilingual or trilingual stenography and typing, the greatest need is for specialists in administration, management, engineering, sanitation, and transportation. There is a demand for experts in agricultural methods, industry, and aviation. North Americans may obtain jobs in these fields, for which there are few qualified natives. Candidates for these jobs must be highly trained and supported by adequate documentation; they must offer acceptable recommendations. Professional degrees and some years of practical experience are usually indispensable for successful consideration.

On the other hand, United States firms have often adopted the policy of training nationals for technical and management positions ... because of the need to conform to labor laws in these countries which stipulate that most of the employees in designated industries be native-born or naturalized citizens.

Our suggestions include the absolute need of a solid knowledge of Spanish and/or Portuguese. The importance of this requirement should not be minimized. Candidates, however, are warned against assuming that knowledge of languages alone will guarantee success in Latin America.

College graduates, particularly those with professional training or experience, have found employment in Latin America through the following agencies, depending on major interest:

- Division of Overseas Information Centers, Department of State, Washington, D.C. Positions may be obtained for the teaching of English, library, supervisory, and administrative work abroad.
- United States citizens may work abroad as members of the Foreign Service (Department of State). The officers in this service are required to be familiar with the civilization and language of the country to which they are sent.
- Specialists may obtain foreign assignments when employed by the United States Department of Agriculture, U.S. Department of Commerce, and the U.S. Justice Department.
- Hundreds of United States firms maintain branches in most Latin American countries. This office (Pan American Union) supplies partial lists of these for many countries. Candidates are urged to write directly to these firms.

BUSINESS OPPORTUNITIES

One of the first steps of entry to an attractive business career is a secretarial job. Bilingual secretaries are in wide demand in various branches of commerce and international relations. Large corporations, airlines, banks, and international organizations maintain foreign departments in which personnel trained in one or a number of foreign languages are needed. The work is interesting and the salaries are always higher than those paid to ordinary secretaries. Furthermore, advancement from a secretarial job to higher positions is rapid.

Closely related to this field are the following types of positions, which also are open to those with bilingual secretarial training: export assistant, assistant foreign credit manager, trade analyst, correspondent, consular invoice clerk, assistant traffic manager, and executive assistant. In recent years, the languages most in demand in connection with these positions have been Spanish, French, and Portuguese.

With the rapidly increasing commercial relations of the United States, there is probably no field today that offers greater opportunity to those who have the training than the import-export field. The pay is good, the work is interesting, and there are also often opportunities for travel.

GOVERNMENT POSITIONS

Aside from positions with commercial businesses, there is a wide variety of interesting activities in the fields of diplomacy and foreign service. The pay is good and there are many possibilities for rapid advancement.

The United States government regularly schedules examinations to supply personnel for the foreign offices of the Departments of State and Commerce. For those who know two languages, there are interesting and well-paying positions as foreign service officers and thousands of jobs as clerks or secretaries in embassies and consulates of the United States. Generally, a college education is not required for the latter positions, and men and women are accepted on the same basis.

The Bureau of Labor Statistics of the U.S. Department of Labor publishes the *Occupational Outlook Handbook,* which contains information on occupations in which "command of a foreign language is either necessary or useful." More than thirty occupations are listed. For each one a reprint is available. Some of the more important of these are as follows:

bookkeeping workers	environmental scientists
secretaries, stenographers, typists	biochemists
banking—bank officers, tellers, clerks	physical scientists, chemists, physicists
advertising, marketing research buyers	physicians
teachers—elementary, secondary, and college	nurses, practical therapists
librarians, library technicians, and assistants	social scientists
civil aviation—pilots, passenger agents	clergy
engineers—civil, mining	social workers
	actors, singers
	newspaper reporters
	interpreters

The reprints may be obtained for a fee at any of the regional offices of the Bureau of Labor Statistics, United States Department of Labor:

1603 JFK Bldg. Boston, MA 02203	P.O. Box 13309 Philadelphia, PA 19101
201 Varick New York, NY 10036	1371 Peachtree Street NE Atlanta, GA 30309

230 South Dearborn Street	525 Griffin Street
Chicago, IL 60604	Dallas, TX 75202
911 Walnut Street	71 Stevenson
Kansas City, MO 64106	San Francisco, CA 94102

The *Occupational Outlook Handbook* may also be purchased from the regional offices or from VGM Career Horizons, NTC/Contemporary Publishing Group, Inc., 4255 West Touhy, Lincolnwood, Illinois, 60646-1975.

ANALYZING JOB OFFERS

If you have succeeded in getting several job offers, each of which seems attractive, the difficult question is: which one should you accept? To make a wise choice, you will have to analyze the demands of the job and evaluate, objectively, your own fitness and eagerness for it. Temperaments and interests differ, and you may be much happier in one position than another.

Of basic importance is knowing exactly what you are expected to do, especially with reference to your linguistic ability. As stated before, competency in a foreign language is on various levels, ranging all the way from a so-called smattering (which may be useful on a lower level) to a high degree of technical skill.

In help-wanted advertisements, the designations most frequently used are "knowledge," "knowledge desirable," "knowledge helpful," "speak," "fluent command," and "can take dictation." As indicated previously, the largest number of office jobs fall under "dictation" and "knowledge."

TYPES OF POSITIONS

Some of the positions for which a person who has had business training and knows a foreign language may qualify are the following:

bilingual stenographer	bookkeeper
consular invoice clerk	assistant trade analyst
export assistant	interpreter

One step higher is that of private secretary. The bilingual stenographer who has taken courses in economics, banking, and law can qualify for the following:

office manager	executive assistant
traffic assistant	assistant production manager
personnel director	interviewer
correspondent secretary	public relations secretary

The last mentioned, that is, public relations, opens up a very broad and attractive field. Related positions are:

international public relations secretary	educational public relations secretary
publicity assistant	industrial relations secretary
public opinion analyst	consumer public relations director
individual campaign public relations secretary	

The most important commercial field for the person with foreign language training is, of course, export-import. Attractive positions are as follows:

export manager	air traffic assistant
assistant manager of foreign department	executive secretary
	trade analyst
supervisor, export department	resident buyer
foreign purchasing agent	foreign field researcher
traffic manager	foreign raw materials buyer
foreign credit manager	translator
international traveling agent	

Then there are the positions for representatives stationed abroad:

business manager	foreign personnel director
foreign markets analyst	export purchasing agent
resident buyer	foreign credit manager

Finally, there are various government positions, here and abroad, that require a knowledge of foreign languages:

diplomatic secretary   foreign service officer
consular assistant   interpreter
foreign markets analyst   foreign representative
raw material analyst

JOB DUTIES

The duties required of you in connection with your work in foreign languages will, of course, depend upon the nature of the business or organization and the responsibilities of your immediate superior.

Since most inexperienced people enter an organization via an office job, let us consider the duties of the stenographer and secretary. The distinction between the two is not always clearly drawn. Secretary means confidential officer and assumes that the knowledge and skills required are above that of the ordinary clerk.

The most important general duties that are required of the average *bilingual secretary* are the following:

- Taking dictation and transcribing shorthand notes. In the case of the bilingual secretary, this means, of course, use of the foreign language when required;
- Composing and writing original letters in English and in the foreign language;
- Receiving callers; acting as interpreter;
- Handling incoming mail, answering letters, and noting information in letters;
- Organizing office routine;
- Organizing filing systems;
- Consulting reference works;
- Making appointments;
- Taking care of telephone calls;
- Keeping minutes of staff and executive meetings;
- Dictating letters; and
- Preparing reports and translating material.

The activities of a *translator* are, of course, quite different. Since all the translator's work will be written, the ability to type is definitely an asset. There will be little need for spoken fluency. On the other hand, the resourcefulness of the translator is important. In the more technical fields of advertising, the translator may even have to coin new words and expressions.

Translating falls into various categories. It may consist of transposing literary material from the foreign language into English. If novels or essays are involved, the translator must possess some literary skill. Or, it may be merely a matter of translating ordinary news dispatches or routine correspondence.

On the other hand, the material may be in highly technical language, as in legal, medical, pharmaceutical, chemical, or engineering articles. Furnishing abstracts is one of the common duties of the translator. The ordinary commercial translation bureau must be prepared for anything, including poorly written and badly phrased material. The more highly paid translators are those who translate English advertising copy into foreign languages, a very delicate task that requires a close knowledge of the culture.

The *interpreter,* too, may work on different levels. At the bottom of the scale is the court interpreter; at the top is the highly gifted UN linguist whose ingenuity is constantly being called upon. The interpreter's effectiveness, of course, depends essentially upon oral fluency.

Oral fluency, too, is involved in all positions requiring personal contacts such as in social work, the hotel and travel business, and nursing.

CHAPTER 5

WORLD TRADE OPPORTUNITIES

America had been a dominant power in world trade for decades. Products from the United States were desired and found in all parts of the globe. It was inevitable that Americans should ask themselves why they should bother learning the language and culture of their trading partners when people abroad wanted American products and services. Besides, their customers knew English anyway, didn't they? The realities began to change with the amazing economic recovery of both of our adversaries in World War II, Germany and Japan. Soon an economic war was being waged, and American business found itself more and more on the defensive. It would surely not be correct to consider our lack of interest in other languages to be the sole cause for this state of affairs, but the general attitude toward other languages and peoples was clearly a major contributing factor. "The American" concept is one that we are still trying to live down. With goods from other countries flooding markets we had previously dominated and with ever-mounting trade deficits, many American multinational companies have begun to realize that employees who also know a foreign language can play an important role in the economic struggle.

IMPORTANCE OF LINGUISTIC TRAINING

That linguistic training is an undeniable asset in this field is affirmed by Lorimer B. Slocum, Director, International Division, Young & Rubicam, one of the largest advertising firms in the United States:

The future looks fairly good. This means that more and more Americans will be needed, both at home and abroad, to serve as salespeople, technicians, teachers, public relations emissaries, troubleshooters, etc. This means that the people of other countries will get to know us better as time goes by, will understand us better, and we hope, like us better.

Students will ask you, "Is it necessary to learn foreign languages?" Maybe they don't *have to,* but they will have a lot more fun if they do, and they will find it easier to achieve their goals. They should remember that the more of a language they know and the more they use it, the friendlier will be their reception....

Yes, there are fine opportunities in the international field for our bright, young, ambitious students and their fresh outlook on life. Their up-to-the-minute information on all branches of business and learning could bring not only a breath of fresh air to near and far places, but also give them a broader outlook on life, while they are doing a good deed for their country.

Words like these, coming from an expert, are extremely encouraging to any young person who plans to enter international trade. They emphasize the importance of foreign language skill, and the significance of the ability to communicate in the international field, as well as the value of innovative new talent to this field.

Although there are many positions open for those who have had only a high school or business school education, preference is given to the college graduate with foreign language fluency for all higher positions. This thought was expressed by D. C. Shirey of the Personnel Department of the Firestone Tire & Rubber Co., Akron, Ohio:

... There is no question that opportunities are great in our company and in many fields of endeavor where a foreign language would be of great assistance.

... There are specific jobs which require specialized education, experience, etc. which open up at various times. In general, Portuguese and Spanish are always good languages to have. The remuneration in the foreign field is, of course, always greater than for similar domestic work.

We feel sure you cannot estimate too strongly the value of foreign languages in the educational requirements for the future where the world is growing smaller every day, and we are constantly coming in closer contact with foreign peoples in all areas in the business world.

Preference is given to the employee with a foreign language proficiency, as pointed out by Bobby J. Schupp of the Overseas Personnel Office of the Standard Oil Company of New Jersey:

> In most of our overseas operations, employment opportunities today are limited primarily to experienced personnel with a background related to the petroleum industry. While the majority of the requirements would be for technical personnel, there are always openings for persons experienced in some particular phase of refining, producing, etc. Practically all of the administrative vacancies are filled from within our company, for here it has been demonstrated that a complete knowledge of company philosophy and policy is essential.
>
> While we do not require a fluency in a foreign language as a prerequisite to employment, we certainly do give consideration to this factor. We stress to all prospective employees the necessity of learning the language of the country in which he or she will be assigned. In some cases, language training will be provided prior to departure for the foreign location, while in others this would be taken care of after arrival. In either situation, company assistance is given.
>
> For an employee to be successful in overseas work, he or she must be conversant with the local language. Both from the social and business standpoints, the employee will soon discover that the ability to speak the language will put her or him in good stead. Much has been said relative to the adjustments that people must make when moving their home to a foreign area. Probably no one factor is more important in making this adjustment than a knowledge of the language.

ADVERTISING

With America's international trade totaling billions of dollars yearly, the worldwide coverage of the best markets through research and advertising is of the utmost importance. In fact, it is so basic to the success of foreign trade that the field of export advertising has been growing by leaps and bounds.

Export Trade has printed a *Directory of Foreign Publications* that have representatives in the United States. About 600 foreign newspapers and magazines are listed, representing the following languages: Spanish,

Portuguese, Dutch, French, German, Italian, Hebrew, Norwegian, Swedish, Turkish, and Hindi.

The same trade journal also provides a list of *U.S. Publications Whose Principal Circulation is in Foreign Countries.* These include technical magazines on antibiotics, automobiles, beverages, office equipment, motion pictures, farm implements, pharmaceuticals, engineering, oil, mechanics, and textiles, and the nineteen international foreign language editions of *Reader's Digest.*

It can readily be seen that the field of export advertising offers great opportunities for those with foreign language training.

EXPORTS

The spread of American big business throughout the world has been phenomenal. Its growth in recent years has slowed somewhat, but it has not been halted, despite various hindrances. *Fortune* magazine in "These Are the Good Old Days" (June 9, 1997) points out that exports have doubled in real terms over the past ten years, to $826 billion (in 1992 dollars).

According to *Forbes* (July 18, 1994) magazine, the top thirty U.S. companies with the largest foreign sales were as follows:

Rank	Company	Non-U.S. Sales ($ million)	Total Sales ($ million)	Foreign as % of Total
1.	Exxon	75,369	97,825	77.3
2.	General Motors	38,646	138,220	28.0
3.	Mobil	38,535	57,077	67.5
4.	IBM	37,013	62,716	59.0
5.	Ford Motor	32,860	108,521	30.3
6.	Texaco	24,292	45,395	53.5
7.	Citicorp	20,762	32,196	64.5
8.	El du Pont de Nemours	16,756	32,621	51.4
9.	Chevron	16,601	40,352	41.1
10.	Proctor & Gamble	15,856	30,433	52.1
11.	Philip Morris Cos.	15,315	50,621	30.3
12.	Hewlett-Packard	10,971	20,317	54.0
13.	American Intl. Group	10,148	20,135	50.4

(continued)

Rank	Company	Non U.S. Sales ($ million)	Total Sales ($ million)	Foreign as % of Total
14.	General Electric	10,036	60,562	16.6
15.	Coca-Cola	9,351	13,957	67.0
16.	Xerox	9,242	19,434	47.6
17.	Digital Equipment	9,152	14,371	63.7
18.	Dow Chemical	8,775	18,060	48.6
19.	United Technologies	8,148	21,081	38.7
20.	Eastman Kodak	7,980	16,364	48.8
21.	Motorola	7,450	16,963	43.9
22.	ITT	7,411	22,762	32.6
23.	Johnson & Johnson	6,935	14,138	49.1
24.	Minn. Mining & Mfg.	6,894	14,020	49.2
25.	PepsiCo	6,712	25,021	26.8
26.	JP Morgan & Co.	6,255	11,941	52.4
27.	Chrysler	5,753	43,600	13.2
28.	Amoco	5,740	25,793	22.3
29.	AT&T	5,576	67,156	8.3
30.	UAL	5,560	14,511	38.3

In Europe, our trade has been greatest with Britain, Germany, and France. The most important languages, besides English, for candidates for European positions in the export and import trade have been German and French. All signs point to the same two languages remaining of paramount importance. As far as the various continents are concerned, our trade is heaviest with countries in the western hemisphere. The top twenty-five U.S. export markets according to *Business America* (April 1994) magazine are:

Rank	Country	1993 Exports ($ billion)
1.	Canada	100.2
2.	Japan	48.0
3.	Mexico	41.6
4.	United Kingdom	26.4
5.	Germany	19.0
6.	Taiwan	16.3
7.	South Korea	14.8

(continued)

Rank	Country	1993 Exports ($ billion)
8.	France	13.3
9.	Netherlands	12.8
10.	Singapore	11.7
11.	Hong Kong	9.9
12.	Belgium-Luxembourg	9.4
13.	China	8.8
14.	Australia	8.3
15.	Switzerland	6.8
16.	Saudi Arabia	6.7
17.	Italy	6.5
18.	Malaysia	6.1
19.	Brazil	6.0
20.	Venezuela	4.6
21.	Israel	4.4
22.	Spain	4.2
23.	Argentina	3.8
24.	Thailand	3.8
25.	Philippines	3.5

According to the *Statistical Abstract of the United States* (1997) issued by the United States Department of Commerce, international investments have grown phenomenally. Nevertheless the trade deficit continues to grow. The following chart, published by the United States Bureau of the Census, lists the major foreign powers with which we trade.

U.S. Exports, Imports, and Merchandise Trade Balance, by Country: 1992 to 1996

Country	Exports, Domestic and Foreign			General Imports[1]		
	1992	1994	1996	1992	1994	1996
Total[2]	448,164	512,670	624,767	532,665	663,768	791,364
Afghanistan	4	5	17	2	6	16
Albania	36	16	12	5	6	10
Algeria	688	1,191	632	1,586	1,525	2,103

(continued)

Country	Exports, Domestic and Foreign			General Imports[1]		
	1992	1994	1996	1992	1994	1996
Andorra	16	5	25	(Z)	(Z)	3
Angola	158	197	268	2,303	2,061	2,687
Anguilla	11	13	13	(Z)	(Z)	1
Antigua	68	65	82	5	5	9
Argentina	3,223	4,466	4,516	1,256	1,725	2,278
Armenia	25	74	57	1	1	2
Aruba	288	274	226	212	462	558
Australia	8,876	9,781	11,992	3,688	3,200	3,855
Austria	1,256	1,373	2,009	1,306	1,749	2,199
Azerbaijan	(Z)	27	54	(Z)	(Z)	5
Bahamas, The	712	685	725	605	203	165
Bahrain	489	443	244	61	155	115
Bangladesh	188	234	210	831	1,080	1,343
Barbados	128	161	222	31	35	41
Byelarus	25	47	53	25	53	52
Belgium	9,775	10,944	12,520	4,476	6,342	6,779
Belize	117	115	107	59	51	68
Benin	27	26	27	10	10	18
Bermuda	242	300	282	7	9	12
Bolivia	222	186	269	162	260	275
Bosnia-Hercegovina[3]	5	39	59	10	5	10
Botswana	47	23	29	12	14	27
Brazil	5,751	8,118	12,699	7,609	8,708	8,762
British Virgin Islands	44	47	54	3	15	7
Brunei	453	376	375	30	46	49
Bulgaria	85	110	138	79	212	126
Burkina	13	7	10	(Z)	(Z)	4
Cameroon	57	54	71	84	55	65
Canada	90,594	114,441	133,668	98,630	128,948	156,506
Cayman Islands	282	202	208	10	53	17
Chad	5	8	3	(Z)	2	7
Chile	2,466	2,776	4,132	1,388	1,822	2,256
China	7,418	9,287	11,978	25,728	38,781	51,495
Columbia	3,286	4,070	4,709	2,837	3,172	4,273
Congo (Brazzaville)	59	38	62	510	403	315
Costa Rica	1,357	1,867	1,814	1,411	1,646	1,974
Croatia[3]	91	147	106	43	115	71
Cyprus	166	209	257	11	18	17
Czechoslovakia	413	(X)	(X)	242	(X)	(X)

(continued)

Country	Exports, Domestic and Foreign			General Imports[1]		
	1992	1994	1996	1992	1994	1996
Czech Republic	(X)	297	410	(X)	316	482
Denmark	1,473	1,215	1,730	1,667	2,122	2,137
Djibouti	11	7	8	(X)	-	(Z)
Dominica	34	26	34	5	7	8
Dominican Republic	2,100	2,800	3,183	2,372	3,094	3,575
Ecuador	999	1,196	1,257	1,343	1,727	1,916
Egypt	3,088	2,844	3,146	435	548	665
El Salvador	742	932	1,072	384	609	1,074
Equatorial Guinea	11	2	17	(Z)	(Z)	76
Estonia	59	33	83	13	29	60
Ethiopia	250	143	148	9	34	35
Federated States of Micronesia	32	25	25	13	13	11
Fiji	59	118	28	67	97	75
Finland	785	1,069	2,438	1,185	1,803	2,345
France	14,593	13,622	14,428	14,797	16,775	18,630
French Guinea	82	196	301	3	3	5
French Polynesia	82	72	88	11	14	17
Gabon	55	40	56	921	1,155	1,949
Gambia	10	4	9	(Z)	2	2
Georgia	16	79	83	7	1	8
Germany	21,249	19,237	23,474	28,820	31,749	38,943
Ghana	124	125	295	96	199	171
Gibraltar	11	23	12	2	4	7
Greece	901	830	820	370	455	496
Greenland	3	3	4	12	10	6
Grenada	24	24	36	8	7	4
Guadeloupe	60	51	66	1	2	1
Guatemala	1,205	1,355	1,564	1,081	1,283	1,673
Guinea	61	50	87	103	92	117
Guyana	118	110	137	102	98	110
Haiti	209	211	474	107	59	144
Honduras	811	1,012	1,641	783	1,097	1,796
Hong Kong	9,077	11,445	13,956	9,793	9,698	9,868
Hungary	295	309	331	347	470	677
Iceland	119	112	257	165	249	236
India	1,917	2,296	3,318	3,780	5,302	6,169
Indonesia	2,780	2,811	3,965	4,530	6,523	8,213
Iran	748	329	(Z)	1	1	(Z)

(continued)

Country	Exports, Domestic and Foreign			General Imports[1]		
	1992	1994	1996	1992	1994	1996
Iraq	1	1	3	-	-	(-)
Ireland	2,862	3,416	3,660	2,262	2,890	4,798
Israel	4,077	5,006	6,009	3,816	5,223	6,426
Italy	8,721	7,193	8,785	12,314	14,711	18,222
Ivory Coast	87	111	141	188	185	397
Jamaica	939	1,066	1,491	599	747	839
Japan	47,813	53,481	67,536	97,414	119,149	115,218
Jordan	258	288	345	18	29	25
Kazakhstan	15	131	138	21	60	114
Kenya	124	170	104	73	109	107
Kiribati	35	23	4	(Z)	1	1
Kuwait	1,337	1,175	1,979	281	1,445	1,640
Kyrgyzstan	2	6	47	1	8	5
Latvia	55	101	165	11	51	99
Lebanon	311	443	627	28	25	42
Lesotho	3	3	3	53	63	65
Liberia	31	46	50	12	4	27
Liechtenstein	12	14	9	36	96	91
Lithuania	44	41	63	5	16	34
Luxembourg	272	228	242	227	288	204
Macao	19	21	30	721	791	858
Macedonia[3]	4	14	14	46	82	125
Madagascar	6	48	12	54	57	46
Malawi	14	19	13	60	57	73
Malaysia	4,363	6,965	8,521	8,294	13,977	17,825
Mali	11	19	18	2	4	6
Malta	58	88	125	91	96	208
Marshall Islands	34	33	29	8	8	5
Martinique	33	31	35	1	4	1
Mauritania	59	14	15	9	4	5
Mauritius	22	24	25	136	217	217
Mexico	40,592	50,840	56,761	35,211	49,493	72,963
Moldova	9	23	22	(Z)	3	30
Monaco	6	6	3	13	18	16
Morocco	496	405	476	178	192	252
Mozambique	150	39	23	19	15	27
Namibia	34	16	22	23	28	27
Netherlands	13,752	13,591	16,615	5,300	6,015	6,617
Netherlands Antilles	478	520	528	644	425	663
New Caledonia	36	27	29	15	23	55
New Zealand	1,307	1,508	1,727	1,219	1,421	1,464

(continued)

Country	Exports, Domestic and Foreign			General Imports[1]		
	1992	1994	1996	1992	1994	1996
Nicaragua	185	186	262	69	167	350
Niger	13	12	27	3	2	1
Nigeria	1,001	509	816	5,103	4,430	5,849
Norway	1,279	1,268	1,558	1,969	2,373	3,869
Oman	257	219	215	186	459	411
Pakistan	881	719	1,277	865	1,012	1,266
Panama	1,103	1,276	1,378	254	323	346
Papua New Guinea	72	65	69	64	108	86
Paraguay	415	794	897	35	80	42
Peru	1,005	1,408	1,767	739	840	1,262
Phillipines	2,759	3,888	6,125	4,355	5,720	8,162
Poland	641	625	968	375	651	627
Portugal	1,024	1,055	960	664	898	1,016
Qatar	189	162	207	70	81	157
Romania	248	337	266	87	195	249
Russia	2,112	2,579	3,340	481	3,235	3,561
Saudi Arabia	7,167	6,011	7,295	10,371	7,687	8,781
Senegal	80	43	56	10	11	6
Singapore	9,626	13,022	16,686	11,313	15,361	20,340
Slovakia	(X)	43	63	(X)	129	124
Somalia	21	30	4	2	(Z)	(Z)
South Africa	2,434	2,173	3,106	1,727	2,030	2,323
South Korea	14,639	18,028	26,583	16,682	19,658	22,667
Spain	5,537	4,625	5,486	3,002	3,554	4,281
Sri Lanka	178	198	211	789	1,093	1,393
Sudan	53	55	50	11	35	19
Suriname	142	122	223	46	43	97
Sweden	2,844	2,520	3,429	4,716	5,044	7,158
Switzerland	4,540	5,614	8,371	5,645	6,376	7,793
Syria	165	199	226	42	64	15
Taiwan	15,250	17,078	18,413	24,596	26,711	29,911
Tajikistan	9	15	17	2	60	33
Tanzania	34	49	50	11	15	19
Thailand	3,989	4,861	7,211	7,529	10,307	11,336
Togo	20	13	20	6	4	4
Trinidad and Tobago	447	541	665	848	1,109	1,017
Tunisia	233	327	189	48	54	76
Turkey	2,735	2,754	2,886	1,110	1,575	1,777
Turkmenistan	35	137	201	1	2	1

(continued)

Country	Exports, Domestic and Foreign			General Imports[1]		
	1992	1994	1996	1992	1994	1996
Turks and Caicos Islands	38	29	44	6	4	5
Uganda	15	28	17	12	35	16
Ukraine	307	181	394	89	327	507
United Arab Emirates	1,553	1,593	2,527	812	449	496
United Kingdom	22,800	26,833	30,916	20,093	25,063	28,892
Uruguay	231	311	484	266	168	260
U.S.S.R. (former)	1,036	(X)	(X)	187	(X)	(X)
Uzbekistan	51	90	352	(Z)	3	157
Venezuela	5,444	4,042	4,741	8,181	8,378	12,903
Vietnam	5	172	616	(Z)	51	319
Western Samoa	73	7	12	1	(Z)	1
Yemen, Republic of	321	178	256	41	183	27
Yugoslavia (former)[3]	167	(X)	(X)	225	(X)	(X)
Yugoslavia, Fed. Rep. of	6	1	46	39	-	8
Zaire	33	40	73	250	188	250
Zambia	68	33	46	70	64	64
Zimbabwe	144	93	91	106	102	133

–Represents zero.   Z Less than $500,000.   X Not applicable.   [1]Imports are on a customs value basis. Exports are f.a.s. value.   [2]Includes revisions not carried to country values; therefore, country values will not add to total.   [3]Beginning June 1992 trade data were reported for the following countries that were formerly part of Yugoslavia—Croatia, Slovenia, Bosnia-Hercegovina, and Macedonia. The Federal Republic of Yugoslavia, which now includes only Serbia and Montenegro, will continue to be shown as "Yugoslavia." Yugoslavia (former) reflects data for the former country and includes data for the period of January through May 1992.

Source: U.S. Bureau of the Census, *U.S. Merchandise Trade,* series FT 900, monthly.

As can be seen from the preceding chart, Asian countries account for a large portion of our foreign trade. Japan ranks one of the highest.

This would lead to the assumption that Japanese would be a language much in demand by American business. But the fact is that very few corporations have seen any great need for their employees to know Japanese in order to compete against them more effectively. This attitude seems to be slowly changing.

With an ever-worsening trade balance picture, the person who has a degree in international business with a strong language component should be in a good position to secure a challenging job.

As has been pointed out, the policy with reference to staffing foreign branches and subsidiaries differs among various firms. Some assume that their representatives will adapt themselves within a short time to conditions in the foreign country, while others subject their foreign representatives to preparatory training before sending them abroad. For the rapid acquisition of a foreign language, they may be sent to a Berlitz school at the expense of the firm.

This is the practice of large international corporations like International Business Machines (IBM). According to an official of this firm, only nationals, that is, natives, are employed in their foreign subsidiaries. In Mexico and Chile, for example, they maintain only one American as manager. In Paris there is a staff of only four Americans. Since the foreign representatives are highly cultured and speak English fluently, there is also very little need for bilingual secretaries.

W. R. Grace & Co.

One of the largest and oldest American export houses is W. R. Grace & Co. Its founding and rapid growth is a success story typical of nineteenth-century America. In 1850 in Ireland, eighteen-year-old William Russell Grace, inspired by seafaring talk of South America, decided to seek his fortune in the land of the Incas. With a group of Irish emigrants he sailed for Callao, Peru, in 1851, and embarked on a business career. It was so successful that he founded W. R. Grace & Co. in 1854. Within a short time this firm achieved preeminence in shipping, banking, air transportation, and manufacturing.

For decades W. R. Grace & Co. was the leading American concern dealing with South America. Within recent years this has changed radically, however, since the firm has withdrawn its major operations from that continent. This was necessitated by a number of unfavorable contingencies but chiefly because of the expropriation of American holdings by the radical governments of Peru and Chile.

The company then transferred its major operations to other parts of the world, dealing with practically every country in Europe, including the former Soviet Union and several of the East European countries. There is also a great volume of business with Australia and Japan.

From a shipping and export house, W. R. Grace has expanded into a number of other fields, which include chemically based products and services; consumer, agricultural, and medical products; and the development of natural resources.

The corporation presently has more than 50,000 employees. The large majority of these are natives of the country in which they work. Relatively few American executives are stationed abroad. There is, however, a continual shuttling back and forth of analysts and specialists from the United States. For them, the knowledge of a foreign language is a great asset. Since the firm no longer devotes its main efforts to South America, many other languages besides Spanish and Portuguese have become important.

OVERSEAS OPPORTUNITIES

The policy of hiring natives of the foreign country for overseas operations is the general policy of firms engaged in international business. M. F. Paul, Employment and Placement Services Manager of IBM World Trade Corporation, said:

> IBM's international operations are managed on a highly decentralized basis. Hiring decisions are made by location IBM management, and the practice is to employ almost exclusively citizens of the countries in which we operate. Occasionally, Americans are hired, but their compensation is based on local economy and payable in local currency. Inquiries that are received in the United States for employment overseas are referred to the respective country personnel departments for their direct handling. The few Americans sent on temporary overseas assignment are experienced IBMers with specific knowledge of IBM's business and its policies and practices.

As indicated, however, by other personnel managers, the knowledge of a foreign language is a highly valuable asset to those sent overseas.

The new employee may be required to spend a year in special training, during which period a base salary is paid and a car is provided.

After an employee has completed preliminary training, an overseas assignment is given. Salary will increase according to responsibility. Frequently, in the case of highly competent foreign trade executives, the annual increases can be very substantial. Bonuses, stock rights, and other fringe benefits can add appreciably to earnings.

On the other hand, the fringe benefits must not be overrated. One foreign employment expert stated:

> True, living allowances for certain areas are added to salaries, but grandiose expense accounts and palatial residences with large staffs of servants are myths of TV-land. A person going abroad will be provided with a sufficient allowance to live as the company expects her or him to live, comfortably and without ostentation. She or he will enjoy prospects of an adequate pension, and the family will have excellent health insurance coverage. The exigencies of foreign living will be taken into account . . .
>
> As an employee's children reach high school or college age, special arrangements are usually made to assure their proper education, including provision for the children's travel to and from the family's overseas home and the United States.

FOREIGN TRADE

In addition to specialized formal training in foreign trade there are other qualifications that play a very important role in every individual's success. They are intelligence, patience, tact, diplomacy, aptitude for languages, cosmopolitan viewpoint, willingness to study, attention to detail and facts, open-mindedness, willingness to put up with discomfort, adaptability, liking for foreigners, and—if married—a mate who also possesses these characteristics.

A good qualification list for successful overseas performance has been published by the United States Bureau of Foreign and Domestic Commerce. It includes the following:

- appearance: well-groomed, appropriate manners, correct speech

- fundamentals of international trade, economics, banking, geography, business, and international law
- thorough knowledge of international trade movements and practices
- thorough knowledge of export trade techniques
- thorough speaking and reading knowledge of at least one foreign language
- residence or travel abroad highly desirable
- intimate knowledge of foreign business practices
- ability to address public gatherings
- ability to write good business correspondence and reports
- knowledge of U.S. resources and familiarity with industrial development in this country in relation to both domestic and export trade

To that list could be added a knowledge of America and its history, Constitution, customs, and current events—including baseball, the World Series, movies, contemporary literature, music, and arts. Americans abroad *are* America to the people with whom they associate. They must have the knowledge and skill to present and defend their valued way of life to the skeptical or misinformed.

There are failures in foreign trade careers. They are caused primarily by a failure to try to understand the people and customs, an inability to accept responsibility, a lack of self-reliance and perseverance, and the failure to identify personal goals with those of the firm.

OVERSEAS ASSIGNMENTS

Professor John Fayerweather, Associate Professor of International Business at the Graduate School of Business of Columbia University, in an article in *Export Trade* entitled "Job Hunting in the Field of International Business Operations," indicates that job opportunities for new college graduates are limited for two reasons. First, most companies are trying to hire local nationals to staff their overseas operations. Second, international posts usually go to those with technical expertise or managerial experience that takes years to develop.

Recent graduates should not give up hope of finding work overseas, however. As the United States expands international investment, more jobs may open up. And new employees with any firm should make their interest in overseas assignments known. Once they have proven their value to the organization, young employees should volunteer for any appropriate international position.

The 1994 edition of the *Directory of American Firms Operating in Foreign Countries* lists 2,600 U.S. corporations operating in 127 countries. There are jobs in international business. But the jobs are widely dispersed, and the requirements for them are often stiff. However, if one invests thought and effort in seeking them out, one can find a good position in a dynamic and interesting field.

CHAPTER 6

GOVERNMENT POSITIONS

The United States federal government is the largest employer in the country. It is also the largest employer of persons equipped with foreign language skills. Most federal employees occupying such positions are employed as translators and bilingual stenographers.

CIVIL SERVICE

In the broad sense of the word, civil servants conduct the various activities of local, state, and federal government offices. Almost one out of every six Americans is a civil servant, and almost every type of work carried on in private business and industry also is found in government service. The range of Civil Service jobs is wide, including carpenters, plumbers, auto mechanics, police officers, doctors, and judges.

In many government activities, an employee may be called upon to use a foreign language. This is particularly true in large metropolitan areas like New York, Philadelphia, Chicago, and San Francisco, where there are large concentrations of foreign-born and minority groups. Within recent years, the need for a knowledge of Spanish has become so urgent that special courses have been arranged for police, doctors, nurses, and social workers.

Formerly, special Civil Service examinations were scheduled for the positions of translator and bilingual stenographer. This has been changed, and at present, the applicant applies directly to the agency for which he or she expects to work. Complete job information and forms may be obtained at any one of the Federal Job Information Centers that are found in all large cities.

DEPARTMENT OF STATE

Charles W. Curtis, while Chief, Recruitment Operations Branch, Division of Personnel, Department of State, wrote:

We are in complete agreement that knowledge of foreign languages is becoming of greater importance to Americans, especially in the international activities of our government.

In the Department of State, there are a number of positions which require foreign language facility. A high degree of language proficiency is a basic requirement for such positions as Information Officer, Cultural Affairs Officer, and Public Affairs Officer in the Information Program in Europe and Latin America. It is also desirable for such positions in the Near and Middle East.

However, other positions in the Department require a higher degree of language proficiency than is ordinarily acquired by traditional academic language training. For example, the Linguistic Scientist employed in our Foreign Service Institute must have a degree in Linguistic Science from an American university, plus teaching experience and professional competence in from one to three languages. The higher salaried positions require a Ph.D. in Linguistic Science in addition to considerable teaching proficiency in at least three languages.

Our Division of Language Service employs Language Typists, Translators, Reviewers, and Interpreters, in approximately the same salary range. Most of the people occupying the positions now have had extensive foreign residence in addition to a thorough academic training. A minimum of two languages is necessary, and the majority of these employees handle four or more. Applicants must have an M.A. or Ph.D. in languages, or an equivalent combination of academic training and pertinent work experience. In either case, without actual work or school experience in a foreign country, applicants generally are unable to satisfactorily pass the qualifying examination given by the Division of Language Services here in Washington. In the Interpreter-Reviewer-Translator category, we mainly use French, Spanish, Portuguese, and some German, Italian, and Russian....

A government bulletin further describes translating jobs in the Department of State as follows:

The Division of Language Services is responsible for all official translating and interpreting services for the Department of State. This includes (a) translation from foreign languages into English and from English into foreign languages; (b) providing interpreting, translating, and related stenographic services for international conferences; (c) reviewing draft treaties before signature to assure substantive conformity between the English and foreign-language texts; and (d) providing escort interpreters for the international educational exchange program and similar programs.

Translators are, as a general rule, asked to translate into their native language. A translator must, therefore, be able to write his native language with a high degree of stylistic skill and have an expert knowledge of the language or languages from which the translations are made. Most translator positions in the Department are for translation into English. Because of the wide range of subject matter involved, the translator must have a very good educational background and broad experience.

Translators into English are usually required to have a fluent knowledge of at least two foreign languages. Translators into foreign languages are required to translate from English into only one language. However, they must be able to write that language with all the skill of a professional writer in the areas where the language is spoken, since practically all such translations are intended for distribution abroad.

The Department's interpreters are called upon to interpret from English into one or more foreign languages or from one or more foreign languages into English at official talks, conferences, or during escort assignments. Both the simultaneous and consecutive systems of interpretation are used. The interpreter must be exceptionally fluent in the languages into which he or she interprets, and her or his speech must be free of any objectionable accent. Like the translator, the interpreter should have a good general educational background, supplemented, if possible, by practical experience in several fields, since the translator may be called upon to handle topics in widely divergent fields.

Note: Simultaneous interpreting is performed as the speech or discussion is proceeding; with consecutive interpreting, the speaker pauses after a certain segment and waits for the interpreter to translate that segment before proceeding with the next segment.

FOREIGN SERVICE

One of the most attractive jobs in the Department of State for a college graduate with skill in a foreign language and a desire to travel is that of a Foreign Service officer.

The following information is taken from a bulletin issued by the Department of State with reference to openings:

> The Department of State is responsible for conducting relations with foreign nations and international organizations; for protecting and advancing political, economic, and other interests of the United States overseas; and for rendering a variety of services to individual Americans abroad. Much of this work is carried out by Foreign Service officers, who, when abroad, serve as diplomatic and consular officers and who, when in Washington, fill most of the more responsible positions in the State Department.
>
> All Foreign Service officers are expected to be well-informed regarding foreign and domestic affairs; be knowledgeable about U.S. government, history, and culture; and be able to speak and write effectively. All officers should be interested in people and have the ability to move easily in business, government, and professional circles.
>
> Competitive examinations are held periodically for appointments as Foreign Service officers or information officers of the United States Information Agency (USIA). The majority of the candidates usually are college graduates, but men and women with professional and vocational experience outside college also are encouraged to take the examination. Professional backgrounds are especially sought by the USIA for its junior officer positions, which increasingly require relevant experience in communications media, cross-cultural communications, American civilization, foreign languages and literature, area studies, and other fields related to the functions of information and cultural affairs officers.

Since the Foreign Service officially represents the United States to other nations, the Department of State and the USIA are particularly interested in recruiting increased numbers of members of minority groups and women. As Equal Employment Opportunity employers, both the Department of State and the USIA adhere to the policy of providing employment opportunities to everyone regardless of race, sex, marital status, religion, or ethnic background.

Upon completion of the examination and selection process, successful candidates are appointed by the President, by and with the consent of the Senate. Usually officers can expect to serve two of their first three tours abroad. A normal tour lasts two years, but may be longer or shorter depending upon conditions at the post and the needs of the Service. Officers are expected to be available for worldwide service, as are their families.

Depending on their qualifications, successful candidates are appointed at Class 6 (in 1997, $27,322 to $40,123) on up to Class 4 ($37,718 to $55,390). New officers serve in probationary status until their first promotion. While officers are abroad, their salaries may be supplemented by quarters allowances, cost-of-living allowances, hardship post differentials, and educational allowances for children, depending on local conditions.

Applicants must indicate whether they wish to be examined for service in one of four functional specializations in the Department of State (administrative, consular, economic/commercial, or political) or in the information/cultural specialty leading to appointment with the United States Information Agency.

ELIGIBILITY REQUIREMENTS

Applicants must be at least twenty-one years of age and citizens of the United States by the date of the written examination. (However, a person twenty years of age as of that date may be examined if the junior year of college has been successfully completed.) There is no upper age limit other than the requirement that a newly appointed officer be able to serve at least one complete tour abroad before reaching the mandatory retirement age of sixty years.

If a candidate is married to a non–United States citizen, the spouse must be naturalized before the candidate can be appointed as a Foreign Service officer.

Applications to take the Foreign Service officer examination for service with the United States Information Agency or the Department of State should be sent to the Recruitment Division, Department of State, P.O. Box 9317, Rosslyn Station, Arlington, Virginia 22209.

EDUCATIONAL PREPARATION

There are no specific educational requirements for appointment to the Foreign Service. However, the written and oral examinations are difficult, and a broad general knowledge is needed to pass them. Moreover, to be an effective representative of the United States abroad, an officer must possess a sound knowledge of the history, government, and culture of the people of the United States, be familiar with foreign and domestic affairs, and be informed regarding current events. Ability to write and speak effectively also is essential.

The best preparation for a Foreign Service career is a good general education, combined with school or practical work experience. Such an education may be obtained at any good undergraduate, graduate, or professional school and might include courses in history, government, economics, literature, and a foreign language. These courses should be supplemented by selective reading of books, newspapers, and journals concerned with current events and foreign affairs.

While language instruction and other training are provided at government expense at the State Department's Foreign Service Institute after appointment, no training, financial aid, or scholarships of any kind are provided beforehand for students and others wishing to prepare themselves for careers in the Foreign Service.

LANGUAGE REQUIREMENT

Knowledge of foreign languages is not required for appointment; but once hired, all new officers must demonstrate professional competency in at least one foreign language prior to the end of their initial probationary period. If necessary, an officer will attend classes at the Foreign Service institute, which offers training in more than forty languages. Those who enter with language abilities are tested within thirty days of appointment and, if found proficient in certain designated languages, may receive a higher salary. The Department of State and the USIA particularly seek persons with knowledge of difficult languages (for example, Arabic, Chinese, Russian). Candidates without prior foreign language ability will be appointed as language probationers, and they must acquire acceptable language competency before tenure can be granted.

CENTRAL INTELLIGENCE AGENCY

Portions of a letter from Mr. Arthur T. McNeil, Coordinator for Academic Affairs of the Central Intelligence Agency (CIA) reveal the extent of its foreign language involvement:

Our recruitment brochures do not stress such [foreign language] opportunities, largely because foreign language skills permeate almost every aspect of our work and we here take them as a given. Very probably we do not appreciate sufficiently that this phenomenon is not altogether self-evident to others. Our reliance on foreign language skills extends to all facets of verbal communication—conversing with native speakers of foreign languages in general as well as in specialized lexicons, often in the scientific and technical fields; reading and translating foreign newspapers, periodicals, scientific/technical journals, manuals, and maps; listening to and transcribing foreign radio broadcasts; translating in reverse, English to foreign languages, for both oral and written communication.

Whenever possible, we prefer to employ people who already possess these skills. However, this is not always possible and, in fact, is becoming increasingly difficult. Consequently, our Agency regularly conducts training programs in approximately twenty-five foreign languages at the basic, intermediate, and advanced levels; we also maintain a capability for teaching, as necessary, a large number of additional languages.

The opportunities we offer to persons with foreign language skills can be full- or part-time, at our Headquarters in the Washington, DC, area or in many locales abroad. Anyone who is interested may write to our Director of Personnel, P.O. Box 1925, Washington, DC 20013; consult a telephone listing of the Central Intelligence Agency recruitment office which we maintain in several major cities in the continental United States; or consult with university/college placement directors about meeting with one of our personnel recruiters on campus or a nearby metropolitan area.

The CIA also employs foreign language instructors with a high level of language competence; a degree in language, linguistics, education, or a related field; and a strong interest in teaching languages to adults. These instructors not only teach, they also develop curricula and help with the preparation of materials.

UNITED STATES INFORMATION AGENCY

The following facts were taken from a brochure issued by the United States Information Agency (USIA):

The USIA is an independent organization within the executive branch and is responsible for the United States Government's overseas information, education exchange, and cultural programs. Since the success of our nation in the international arena depends on whether, and how well, our actions and intentions are understood by the rest of the world, the work of this agency assumes great importance.

Personal contact is foremost among the USIA's means of communication. Agency officers overseas are on the front lines of telling America's story to the world. Not only are they in contact with foreign leaders, but they also advise American ambassadors.

The Agency also uses international cultural and academic exchanges, including the Fulbright program; media products such as direct satellite transmissions of remarks by the President and . . . chief advisors; films, videotapes, magazines, books, and newsfile, plus direct broadcasts by its radio service, the Voice of America, to carry out its mission overseas.

Over 900 Agency officers are employed at 205 posts in 126 countries. The officers are aided by some 3,500 locally hired nationals who operate the libraries, show the films, translate the texts, and display the exhibits. Another 3,400 employees serve in the United States, half of whom are engaged in the broadcasting operations of the Voice of America.

The full range of editorial techniques is employed for the coverage of current events. The agency publishes press reports for foreign language publications in English, French, Spanish, and Arabic. USIA posts overseas produce ten magazines in eighteen languages.

The Agency operates numerous libraries and reading rooms, and it maintains 120 cultural centers abroad. The facilities attract millions of visitors annually.

Requirements for the career intern program include a college degree or equivalent in communications, radio–T.V., broadcasting, journalism, foreign affairs, government, and foreign languages. In general the special skills that are helpful for careers with the Voice of America include the ability to speak and write a foreign language fluently, the possession of a voice suitable for radio broadcasting, and experience in radio writing, editing, or producing.

IMMIGRATION AND NATURALIZATION SERVICE

The New York District of the Immigration and Naturalization Service maintains a staff of interpreters who do the interpreting and translating in connection with immigration matters. The positions are under the Civil Service and are filled in accordance with current laws and regulations.

Abraham Wassner, the Supervising Director of the Interpreter Section of the U.S. Immigration Service, had this to say about his department:

The staff consists of regular, permanently appointed interpreters and of interim interpreters ... A much larger number of part-time interpreters is hired on a per diem basis ... The regular interpreters are on a standard annual wage scale, according to their grade.

The interpreting service is not confined to the New York office; it extends to many parts of the world. Offices are maintained in Paris, Frankfurt, Athens, the Virgin Islands, and Montreal. Service is also provided throughout the United States by telephone, since the interpreter 'is heard but need not be seen.' Stations are maintained in New Orleans, San Francisco, and other cities of the West.

Twenty-nine principal languages are used, but a great many rare and exotic languages, as well as dialects and even jargon, are called for. The very names of some of these are now generally familiar, as for instance, Khmer (Cambodia), Twi (Gambia), and Gujarati (India). The little known languages and dialects, of which almost a hundred are listed, are the ones for which it is difficult to find competent interpreters. Within a year about a hundred extra personnel are hired for such languages. As far as the standard major languages are concerned, there is no difficulty at all; plenty of capable linguists are available. After selecting the interim interpreters, the Director trains them and gives them their assignments.

The staff of interpreters is, of course, highly trained and well experienced. All of them speak a number of languages. In addition, many of the Immigrant Inspectors and Investigators have competence in one or more of the more common languages. This is definitely an asset in dealing with people coming from so many foreign countries. Officers in these categories have been promoted to the highest ranks of the service. As an administrative assistant says, although it cannot be said that their promotion was because of a language ability, certainly it was not a hindrance. One of the major divisions of the Immigration and Naturalization Service is the Border Patrol. This body of highly trained officers has as its most important activity "linewatch": the detection, prevention, and apprehension of illegal aliens. Since the major area of concern is the United States–Mexican border, interested persons must learn to read and speak Spanish if they do not already possess this ability. Additional credit is given to those applicants who already have these skills when applying.

DEFENSE

Foreign languages play an important role in the Department of Defense, which includes the Army, Navy, Air Force, and Marine Corps. The foreign operations by the various branches require the services of many individuals with foreign language skills. At present, 15,000 military positions have documented needs for foreign languages. To provide for these needs, special language schools have been established.

The Defense Language Institute of the Army, which teaches forty languages to military personnel, has over 900 civilian faculty and academic staff positions in curriculum development, teaching, and testing foreign languages at the Foreign Language Center in Monterey, California. Native speakers are preferred as instructors, but a limited number of American-born instructors are also hired. The positions are at GS-7 level. The minimum language requirement is described as follows:

> The applicant must have speaking proficiency of the target language equivalent to that of an educated native speaker, free from undesirable accents or defects. He or she must have the ability to write the language with accurate sentence structure and proper expression of ideas, and possess the ability of stylistic discrimination.

The training academies of the armed forces employ regular foreign language teachers in their foreign language departments. The Air Force Academy offers instructors in Arabic, Chinese, French, German, Japanese, Russian, and Spanish.

At the United States Military Academy at West Point, New York, instruction is offered in Arabic, Chinese, French, German, Portuguese, Russian, and Spanish. The department is staffed by regular or reserve Army officers on active duty, including a few native-born speakers. The National Guard and Reserves also provide linguists in emergencies. Military linguists may earn up to $100 extra pay per month.

NATIONAL SECURITY AGENCY

An agency of the Department of Defense, the National Security Agency (NSA) coordinates domestic and foreign communications affairs. The NSA collects and analyzes foreign electromagnetic signals, protects U.S. telecommunications and computer systems against exploitation, and trains U.S. government organizations to better secure their own operations. It also develops code and cypher systems. To carry out its missions, NSA makes use of highly sophisticated technologies. Its linguists increasingly use computerized dictionaries and glossaries. Analysts can query an ever-expanding political, military, and economic database to help them analyze current situations.

NSA has special need for Asian, Middle Eastern, or Slavic language majors. At NSA, linguists are able to constantly improve their linguistic skills and apply their knowledge of culture and politics to the analysis of current intelligence information. Their work is described as follows:

Specific duties include translating technical materials into English; transcribing and/or summarizing spoken materials; and compiling linguistic aids such as glossaries, handbooks, and the results of language analysis. Other assignments could include preparing grammars or courses for poorly documented languages, teaching foreign languages, or working in peripheral fields such as computer applications to linguistic problems. Individual assignments are varied and may be highly specialized, involving in-depth research. Fluency in the spoken language is generally not required, but familiarity with modern idiomatic and colloquial speech is essential. Excellent English skills are also necessary...NSA is committed to the career development of its employees. All new employees receive a combination of formal and on-the-job training to provide a smooth entrance to the NSA workforce. Numerous people are available for career counseling and training information throughout an employee's career.

The National Cryptologic School is the Agency's on-site training facility. It offers a broad range of classes—language, technical, and management, with both traditional and self-paced instruction—for individual development. There are also varied opportunities for graduate study. Part-time study is available with full tuition support at any of the many nearby universities and colleges, including the University of Maryland, Johns Hopkins, and Georgetown. Employees may also be eligible for full-time graduate study programs, as well as other long-term training programs, with full tuition and salary support. NSA also encourages membership in professional organizations and participation in their conferences and symposia throughout the country.

FEDERAL BUREAU OF INVESTIGATION

The FBI advertises its need for linguists in the following terms.

The FBI needs linguists with ability in a wide range of languages including, but not limited to: Arabic, Bulgarian, Chinese, Czech, Farsi, Greek, Japanese, Korean, Polish, Punjabi, Serbo-Croatian, Spanish, Russian, and Vietnamese.

The FBI has an urgent need for translators. There are three types of job opportunities offered: Special Agent Linguists; Language Specialists, who are employed full-time; and Contract Linguists, who are self-employed and work on an hourly basis.

Special Agent Linguists may be involved in every phase of important investigative work, which might include surveillance, interviewing witnesses and suspects, apprehending fugitives and criminals, collecting evidence, providing testimony in court, and other duties. Working as a Special Agent Linguist might require monitoring a court-authorized wiretap in a drug case, examining business records to investigate white-collar crime, collecting evidence of espionage activities, blocking terrorist activity, or handling sensitive undercover assignments.

The translating work of Language Specialists and Contract Linguists is primarily document-to-document or audio-to-document. The subject matter may be in any area in which the FBI, the investigative arm of the United States Department of Justice, has jurisdiction, including: investigations into organized crime, white-collar crime, public corruption, financial crime, fraud against the government, bribery, copyright matters, civil rights violations, bank robbery, extortion, kidnapping, air piracy, terrorism, foreign counterintelligence, interstate criminal activity, fugitive and drug trafficking matters, and other violations of federal statutes.

DRUG ENFORCEMENT AGENCY

Another agency now in need of services for a number of foreign languages is the Drug Enforcement Agency (DEA), which operates worldwide to combat international narcotics smuggling. Because of stepped-up activities on the part of Central and South American drug smugglers, there is a special need for agents who can speak Spanish and understand the dialects of these regions. Other areas of concern are Southeast Asia and, increasingly, the Middle East. DEA agents with language skills work overseas with U.S. embassies as intelligence research specialists, general investigators, or administrative or clerical employees. The DEA offers bonuses to employees with high levels of proficiency in the languages of the areas to which they are assigned.

UNITED NATIONS

Most of the nearly 3,000 employees of the United Nations (UN) are stationed at the organization's headquarters in New York City. The UN offers many attractive and interesting openings to trained linguists. The positions extend over a wide range, from the bilingual typist at the bottom to the highly skilled, rapid-fire interpreters at the top. The Chief of the Overseas Recruitment Section says:

> The language posts of the United Nations Secretariat consist of translation, interpretation, verbatim reporting, summary reporting, proofreading, clerical, and secretarial. Arabic, Chinese, English, French, Russian, and Spanish are the official languages of the organization, and out of these, English and French are considered as the working languages. Hence, staff may be needed to work in the capacities enumerated above in one or more of the specified languages.

The following data are taken from a circular issued by the United Nations entitled *General Information on United Nations Employment Opportunities:*

> The United Nations has a steady need for competent staff in various fields. While it is impossible to list in detail the different types of positions for which the organization recruits, the major categories of staff are described below. The majority of professional posts in the Secretariat are closely related to the nature of the work required by Resolutions of the General Assembly and its principal organs. As a result, the need is largely for specialized professional candidates, with a concentration in economics and related fields. Preference is given to candidates with a knowledge of both working languages of the Secretariat, that is, English and French. In addition to professional personnel, there is a continuous need for

stenographic help and linguistic staff, such as translators and interpreters, who are not subject to geographical distribution considerations.

Professional Posts.   The professional vacancies that occur periodically call for persons of real professional talent in fields related to the work of the United Nations. A Junior professional candidate must have an advanced university degree. For higher-level professional posts, candidates are expected to have relative and meaningful professional experience.

Technical Assistance Experts.   The United Nations Programmes of Technical Cooperation are administered by the United Nations. Personnel requests are usually for senior expert advisers, who are required to have reached the highest professional standing after long experience in their fields.

Administrative Posts.   Administrative vacancies are few and far between and, in any case, are normally filled by the reassignment of existing staff.

Public Information Posts.   Applications for appointments in the Office of Public Information are particularly numerous and, consequently, competition is keen. Preference is given to candidates able to work in more than one of the official languages.

Posts in the Office of Legal Affairs.   The Office of Legal Affairs has a relatively small staff. Only candidates with specialization in public international law are considered, and preference is given to those with a working knowledge of both English and French or Spanish.

Translator/Precis-Writers.   Recruitment is by annual competitive examination and interview. A candidate is required to translate from at least two official languages (Arabic, Chinese, English, French, Russian, and Spanish) into her or his main language. Translators, with the exception of those in the Arabic, Chinese, and Russian Sections, are also required to serve as precis-writers.

Interpreters.   Interpreters are recruited by individual examination. They are required to interpret into their native language, which should be one of the six official languages of the UN, and must have full auditory comprehension of at least two of the other official languages. Candidates may either be trained interpreters, capable of passing the qualifying examination immediately, or they may be persons of suitable linguistic and general cultural background (a university degree is required) who can be trained to meet the required standard in a few weeks or months.

Librarians. Candidates for librarian posts in the Secretariat must have a degree from a recognized library school or an equivalent professional qualification and possess at least a reading knowledge of several languages, plus two or three years' professional experience.

Clerical and Secretarial Posts. Most vacancies are for secretaries and typists, preferably bilingual (English plus French or Spanish). Graduation from high school, or the equivalent, is required. The minimum requirements for secretarial posts are a typing speed of 50 to 60 words per minute and a stenographic speed of approximately 100 words per minute.

Guides. Guides are recruited on a local basis, usually once a year, and begin their training early in March. They must be fluent in English and any other language, with a good speaking voice.

In addition to the positions already named, the following jobs also are available, many of which require a foreign language: social welfare personnel; demographers and population personnel; computer programmers; specialists in economics, statistics, sociology, and industrial development for UN posts outside the headquarters area; UN Field Service personnel; military personnel and observers; and personnel for the various specialized agencies of the United Nations.

Persons who wish to be considered for employment at the UN should address an application to the Office of Personnel Services, United Nations, New York, NY 10017.

Translator/Precis-Writer

The duties of English Translator/Precis-Writer are: (a) to translate into English, for the most part from French, Russian, or Spanish, but occasionally from Arabic, Chinese, and other languages, documents relating to various aspects of United Nations activities, including political debates; economic, social, and legal reports; international agreements; scientific and technical studies; and official correspondence; and (b) to attend meetings of United Nations bodies and draft summary records of their proceedings.

Candidates must be native speakers of English and graduates of a university or an equivalent establishment where the language of instruction was preferably their mother tongue. "Mother tongue" is defined as the language in which the candidate has completed the essential part of her or his education and in which he or she writes correctly, with style and with a rich vocabulary reflecting a university-level education.

Candidates must have a perfect command of English, a thorough knowledge of French and one other official language (Arabic, Chinese, Russian, or Spanish). A knowledge of other languages is a valuable additional qualification.

The written examination lasts two days and consists of (1) translation into English of a French text of a general nature (3 hours); (2) translation into English of two French texts of a technical nature, chosen by the candidate from the five offered (3 hours); (3) summary in English of a French speech (2 hours); and (4) translation into English of two additional texts to be selected out of eight offered from another of the four official languages (2 hours).

Candidates who are successful in the written examination will be interviewed ten to twelve weeks after the examination by a Board of Examiners. The interview is an integral part of the examination, and candidates who are called should not assume that they will automatically be offered an appointment. The Board will recommend to the Assistant Secretary-General the most suitable candidates for appointment. Travel expenses to and from the place of interview will be reimbursed by the United Nations.

Examinations for English Translator/Precis-Writer are normally held in the spring in a number of designated cities, including Geneva, London, Vienna, and New York. Candidates should apply to the Office of Personnel Services, United Nations, New York, NY 10017.

Interpreter

A special circular issued by the United Nations office entitled *Information for Persons Interested in Examinations for Interpreters* contains the following information:

- Candidates for the post of a United Nations interpreter are required to pass an examination to ascertain their professional skill and proficiency in rendering orally from one language to another speeches made at the United Nations meetings. Those considered for regular appointments (rather than temporary assistance) also are required to pass a general culture test designed to assess their educational background of world events and history, with particular emphasis on political, economic, and social questions of interest to the United Nations. Tests are arranged individually at Headquarters in New York or at the United Nations office in Geneva for candidates found eligible on the basis of their credentials and preliminary interview.
- United Nations interpreters must have a thorough knowledge of at least three of the Organization's official languages (Arabic, Chinese, English, French, Russian, and Spanish). As a rule, they interpret into their native tongue and must have full auditory comprehension of at least two of the other official languages. This linguistic knowledge must cover a wide variety of fields—political, economic, legal, literary, etc. Mere ability to converse socially in several languages is not enough.
- Besides linguistic knowledge and skill, United Nations interpreters must be so equipped by education and experience that they have a thorough understanding of the various subjects debated in any of the meetings to which they may be assigned—or at least the intellectual ability to acquire this understanding by study. Candidates are therefore expected to be graduates of a university or an equivalent establishment.
- Interpreters normally are offered a probationary appointment at the P-2 level. After two years of satisfactory service they are offered a permanent contract and promoted to the P-3 level, in which there are thirteen steps, each representing an annual increment. In exceptional cases appointment may be at the P-3 level. In some cases a fixed-term contract may be offered instead of a probationary appointment. Competent interpreters are eventually promoted to the P-4 level, in which there are twelve steps.

Verbatim Reporter

The following information is given with reference to the position of verbatim reporter for the UN.

NATURE OF THE WORK

All verbatim reporting at the United Nations is what is often called "immediate copy." The transcript of a given meeting must be completed or ready for dispatch to the reproduction shop not more than one and one-half hours after the end of the proceedings. This is necessitated by the rules of procedure of most United Nations bodies, which call for the distribution of the complete record to all delegations within twenty-four hours, and time must be left for the processes of reproduction, collation, and distribution of many hundreds of copies.

Consequently, the official verbatim record of a body such as the General Assembly is taken by a team of reporters numbering not fewer than eight (and sometimes more), who normally work on a timetable of ten-minute takes. For a meeting beginning at 3:00 P.M., for instance, the first reporter takes notes until 3:10, is relieved by a colleague who records from 3:10 to 3:20, and so on until all have had ten minutes of note-taking. In the meantime each, in turn, returns to the typing room and dictates to a typist, who types the transcript. Each reporter must finish dictating the first take in time to return to the meeting for a second, and so on. Thus with eight reporters each has seventy minutes in which to dictate the notes and proofread the transcript of each ten-minute take. The reporter may have to record speeches made in English as well as the English interpretations of speeches made in the other five official languages. In this manner, most United Nations bodies have verbatim records prepared simultaneously in English, French, Spanish, Russian, and sometimes Arabic.

QUALIFICATIONS

A candidate for a post of verbatim reporter at the United Nations is expected to have a university degree and to give proof of ability to take notes at not less than 180 words per minute (shorthand or stenotype and transcribe them accurately. Since many of the speeches are made by persons who do not speak English as their native tongue, the verbatim reporter also is expected to be able to edit her or his notes while dictating so that at least the grosser errors of grammar and syntax are eliminated without doing violence to the meaning. Further, the verbatim reporter must verify and correct, if necessary, all quotations included in speeches, put in references to documents, and be able to spot and correct whatever errors of fact speakers may make, or at least, recognize them as such and bring them to the attention of the chief of the service.

There are as many different accents to cope with as there are delegations, and a quick ear is essential. The reporter is also expected to be familiar in a general way with international affairs and with the history and organization of the United Nations. A knowledge of at least one of the other official languages (Arabic, Chinese, French, Russian, or Spanish) is very helpful. Since the material dealt with may range over many different technical subjects, the reporter can hardly have too large a vocabulary or too wide a sphere of knowledge, even if only in general terms. Finally, the reporter must be ready to work at any time of the day or night, on Saturdays, and even on Sundays, often at very short notice, whenever meetings are held.

ARABIC VERBATIM REPORTERS

These reporters work in New York during the General Assembly session only. Candidates for these positions should have a university degree with Arabic as their main language. They must be able to record the minutes of meetings at a speed of not less than 140 words per minute, and they must have a knowledge of at least one of the other official languages.

Salary and Benefits for the Professional Staff

Professional positions (1996) are graded from P-1 to P-5 depending on the candidate's experience and education. A P-1 salary level ranges from about $19,200 to $27,200; P-2 from about $25,200 to $34,800. Gross salaries are subject to Staff Assessment, which operates much like an income tax, the whole amount of the tax being withheld at the source. Each monthly salary check is, therefore, a "net" figure. In the event that the United Nations salary is legally subject to national income tax as well as Staff Assessment, the United Nations will generally refund to the employees the amount of such income taxes payable in respect to their United Nations salaries.

Staff members may also be entitled to the following additional benefits, subject to specific terms of appointment and to the provisions of the UN Staff Rules and Regulations:

- installation and repatriation grants
- dependency allowance
- education grants for dependent children
- membership in the United Nations Joint Staff Pension Fund
- six weeks' leave a year (which may be accumulated up to a maximum of twelve weeks)
- travel costs for themselves and their families on joining the United Nations, on home leave (every two years), and on repatriation after service

Secretary, Stenographer, Typist, and Clerk

The only vacancies in the secretarial category open to outside applicants are at junior levels (age limits eighteen to thirty-five). Openings at senior levels are filled by promotion.

All applicants are required to take entrance examinations held weekly at the United Nations General Recruitment Section, located at One UN Plaza, Forty-fourth Street and First Avenue, New York City. These examinations are given in the six official languages of the UN at the choice of the candidate. They are scheduled some time in advance. Interviews are conducted between 10:00 A.M. and 12:30 P.M., Monday to Friday, in Room DC 1-200. As vacancies occur, selection is made from a roster of successful candidates.

Examinations are given for clerks, typists, stenographers, and bilingual secretaries. The examinations for bilingual secretaries, stenographers, and typists include the following requirements: Languages—English/French and English/Spanish. Standards required in the candidate's best language are as follows:

Secretary and Stenographer—general aptitude test, 90 wpm shorthand, 50 wpm typing.

Typist—general aptitude test, 50 wpm typing.

Standards required in the candidate's *second* language:

Secretary and Stenographer—general aptitude test, 75 wpm shorthand, 45 wpm typing.

Typist—general aptitude test, 45 wpm typing.

Technical qualifications of candidates are tested in group examinations. Candidates also may be asked to draft a short letter in both languages.

Education. Graduation from a high school or equivalent. Background and work experience determine the starting salary.

Medical Examination. All appointments are subject to the successful passing of the medical examination, normally given at United Nations Headquarters.

Salary. Salary varies according to background and experience. In addition, certain allowances and benefits, such as pension fund, medical insurance, and sick leave, are available under the United Nations Staff Regulations and Staff Rules. Annual leave accrues at the rate of two and one-half days a month, or thirty working days a year.

Opportunities for Advancement. The scale of salaries comprises five grade levels with nine to ten steps in each grade. Annual within-grade increments are given on the basis of satisfactory service. Promotions are based on merit and length of service.

Overseas Mission Assignment. A staff member with a permanent appointment (normally granted after two years of service) who has reached the age of twenty-three may apply for a mission assignment. The United Nations has field missions in many parts of the world.

Language Instruction. Free language courses in the six official languages (Arabic, Chinese, English, French, Russian, and Spanish) are available, and staff members are encouraged to enroll in them. Successful completion of the course entitles the staff member to a special language allowance. In cases in which a staff member is proficient in two of the official languages, an additional allowance is given for proficiency in a third language.

United Nations Guides

While it was previously only strongly recommended that an official UN guide know a second language in addition to English, it now is listed as a prerequisite for that position. Guides must be between the ages of twenty and thirty, with a college education or equivalent. It is their task to guide visitors on tours through the United Nations Headquarters.

Guides are expected to conduct four, possibly five, tours a day. They work five days a week, including Saturdays and Sundays and holidays on a rotating basis. In addition, there are some half-time guides, who work twenty hours a week, again including weekends.

The initial salary is approximately $12 an hour. Half-time guides earn one-half of this amount. Initial appointment is for a probationary period of three months. There is a short paid training period. Annual leave is thirty working days a year.

Candidates must be fluent in English, with a good speaking voice. They should have a college education or the equivalent. Some study in economics, international affairs, political science, or an interest these fields is desirable. Applicants who are offered employment must complete a satisfactory medical examination before their appointment can be confirmed.

Guides are recruited on a local basis once a year and begin training during the early part of March. A personal interview at Headquarters is required during the annual recruitment campaign. For the recruitment of candidates, the United Nations does not use commercial employment agencies. Qualified candidates are, therefore, invited to apply directly to their New York offices.

PEACE CORPS

The Peace Corps is an extremely interesting opportunity for young people who are ready to serve as volunteers in the improvement of international relations and who are eager to live in a foreign country. The Peace Corps works in the areas of education, health, home economics, agriculture, natural resource preservation, urban development, and small business assistance.

Since 1961, Peace Corps volunteers have shared their skills and trained people in developing nations around the world. In many instances, Peace Corps volunteers are the only Americans living and working as a part of local communities in these countries. They gain credibility and prove effective because they speak the language of the people, appreciate local customs, and adapt to living and working conditions that are often considerably different from those at home.

Peace Corps volunteers strive to create mutual understanding between Americans and the people with whom they are living and working. More than 6,500 volunteers serve today in over 90 countries. Their experience is in general a satisfying one; in regular surveys of volunteers, a vast majority say they would gladly serve again.

Peace Corps volunteers must be United States citizens, eighteen years or over, in good health, and willing to serve abroad for at least two years. Every applicant must submit to a medical examination and a legal background check. Although competence in a foreign language is not an absolute requirement, it is, of course, a great asset. French or Spanish are particularly desirable. For those without knowledge of the language of the area they will serve, language training is provided on arrival in the country in eight- to ten-week sessions, along with technical and cultural preparation. This provides survival and social skills on which volunteers can build. Essential for Peace Corps service are a college degree and a skill in one of more than 300 categories. These include accountancy, agriculture, fisheries, forestry, engineering, business, health, education, English as a foreign language, plumbing, nursing, and certain skilled trades such as carpentry, welding, masonry, and auto/diesel mechanics.

As well as training for the two-year assignment, medical care and transportation also are provided. The monthly subsistence allowance covers food, lodging, and incidentals. There is no salary. At the end of the service the volunteer receives a readjustment allowance of $200 for every month served, including the training period, a total of $5,400 (in 1992). Forty-eight days vacation are granted.

In the foreign country, the volunteers work for a government department or agency, under the supervision of local officials. They speak the language of the people and are subject to local laws.

One very important area is teaching. Assignments are as varied as the cultures in which they operate. Some volunteers teach in major cities; others in rural areas. Volunteers are needed for almost every field of education—elementary, secondary, and college level; commercial; health; and special education. Many of those who teach on a secondary level teach math, science, or English as a foreign language (EFL).

Teaching EFL in the Peace Corps

EFL volunteers are expected to have a degree in English, TEFL, linguistics, French or some other foreign language, or education, with a concentration in one of these areas, and certification or experience in teaching or tutoring EFL or a foreign language. Ability to speak a second language is valued. Preferred candidates have usually demonstrated leadership in community or youth group activities or have gardening experience or health certification and experience.

According to the Peace Corps:

> Volunteers work in a broad range of assignments. They teach in secondary schools, and train teachers in teachers' colleges, universities, and on-the-job in elementary and secondary schools. They develop curricula and compile textbook materials. They serve as resources, consultants, and advisors. And they work in a variety of settings, traditional urban or rural classrooms, government ministries, or even traveling workshops.... In addition, many volunteers take on secondary projects in their spare time, cultivating example-setting vegetable gardens, coaching sports after school, coordinating community development projects with neighbors, or

teaching improved health and nutrition practices to village women and children.... (They) receive training and experience that (makes them) very attractive to future employers. School systems, educational corporations, and international organizations value the skills of returned education volunteers.... (They) also receive a number of other more tangible benefits, including partial cancellation or deferment of some government-sponsored student loans, comprehensive language and cross-cultural training,... possible academic credit from the National PONSI program of the Regents of the State University of New York, and opportunities for scholarships and fellowships for master's degree programs in colleges and universities throughout the U.S.

Application may be made to the Peace Corps of the United States, Box 941, Washington, DC 20526. The Peace Corps service is so many-sided and fascinating that one may say that it is not just a preparation for a career, but a preparation for life. After their return, many volunteers have continued in jobs in which they can use their language skills.

CHAPTER 7

SPECIAL VOCATIONS

In addition to the positions where linguistic training is of prime importance, there are many other activities in which a supplemental knowledge of a foreign language is useful and highly desirable. There are also certain professional or business undertakings in which a given linguistic proficiency is basic; for example, reading ability for librarians and research workers, and speaking ability for radio broadcasters.

Here are a number of specialized vocations in which foreign languages are extremely useful.

ADVERTISING

International advertising is a highly specialized activity. Its prime purpose, of course, is to promote the sale of American products overseas. Since the latter are sold throughout the world, all of the major and some of the lesser languages are of importance in the field of advertising.

Joseph W. Madden, Executive Vice President of National Export Advertising Service, Inc., said:

> In the important world markets today, English has become the businessperson's language. Consequently, it is possible to conduct a relatively satisfactory business meeting in English.
>
> In order to forge lasting friendships, and therefore more successful long-term business results, a knowledge of the particular country's lan-

guage is essential. Even the simple willingness to use the local language (however badly) is welcomed—and the "stranger" more readily becomes a friend. Fluency in the local languages, of course, greatly facilitates the whole process of establishing a mutually profitable business arrangement.

AIRLINES

All American airlines flying to foreign countries require at least part of their personnel to know a foreign language. The educational director of a leading overseas airline, as quoted in *Vocational Opportunities for Foreign Language Students,* said:

Airway routes go to all countries around the world. Employees who are sent to those other countries, of course, have to be able to speak the language of the country, and this means that we have to have employees who speak Spanish, French, German, and Portuguese and, in some cases, still other languages. Pilots generally are qualified in a foreign language and, on many routes, knowledge of a foreign language is required for stewards. In Latin America they have to be able to speak Spanish because many of their passengers speak no other language.

On most of the airlines crossing the Atlantic, flight attendants make announcements in three languages. Dr. John H. Furbay, Director, Air World Education, TWA, commented:

Americans serving in other countries should be able to speak the languages of those countries, or suffer a great reduction in the effectiveness of their own activities. All hostesses, district managers, and others who meet the public abroad must know the language of countries to be served.

AUTO INDUSTRY

Most of the large American automobile manufacturers have export divisions and maintain agencies abroad. In a number of instances, they have technical and commercial arrangements with foreign companies. Ford, for instance, has its own plants in Germany and turns out a special model for that country. American cars are seen all over the world.

The vast majority of employees in overseas operations divisions are nationals of the country in which the plant is located. A few important American representatives of the company are assigned to overseas posts. These individuals must be fluent in the foreign language. With reference to such assignments the Director of Personnel of General Motors Overseas Operations comments:

> When one of our U.S. employees is chosen for an overseas assignment, we provide language training for the employee and her or his family as part of the pre-assignment orientation offered. The amount of such training will vary with individuals, depending upon the extent of prior knowledge and their ability to absorb the training.

The International Personnel Coordinator of Chrysler Corporation states that his company requires a foreign language for candidates in their international training program. An employee without language skills assigned to an overseas position is given the opportunity of learning the language in the foreign country.

The Goodyear Tire & Rubber Company, like many other large firms, provides language training for its employees in the international field.

BANKING

In recent years many large banks have set up special departments to handle their foreign interests. It has been found necessary to maintain staffs that are linguistically competent to handle the great volume of communications. Large institutions like the Chase Manhattan Bank and Citibank work extensively in languages such as French, Spanish, German, Italian, and Russian. Translation divisions deal with the other languages in which business operations are of smaller volume. For these positions employees are preferred who have a working knowledge of several languages.

Several large banks maintain branches abroad, including the Chase National Bank and the National City Bank. In big cities there are a number of foreign banks. These, of course, have a direct need for linguistically trained personnel. Emilio Mayer of the Banca Commerciale Italiana wrote:

> Quite frequently we receive inquiries from banks or other firms engaged in foreign trade seeking office help with a knowledge of foreign languages. The inquiries pertain to receptionists, secretaries, clerks, department heads, and officers, and the languages most in demand are Spanish, Italian, French, and German.
>
> It has been my experience that the request greatly exceeds the supply, especially if a thorough knowledge of the language is required. It seems to me that the knowledge of a foreign language gives an immediate advantage to anyone seeking a job. Furthermore, the chances for advancement are far greater, not to mention the pleasant possibility of travel abroad.

However, as has been pointed out previously, the number of positions in certain fields is limited, and the linguistic ability must go hand in hand with some other technical skill.

This is stressed by Harmon Martin, Personnel Department, The First National City Bank of New York, who stated:

> ...Our firm practically never requires a language as a condition of employment except for a very few places in our Translators Department. At the present moment this bank has fewer than 200 American citizens scattered among its 4,500 employees in our overseas branches.

BROADCASTING

For radio announcers the ability to speak or at least read a foreign language or two is a definite asset. Most announcers on the big stations do possess this ability, for they are called on every day to pronounce correctly the titles of classical musical selections, the names of operas, the names of foreign celebrities, geographical place names, and occasional quotations in a foreign language. The radio announcers on local foreign language programs in Italian, Yiddish, German, Polish, and Spanish are usually persons of foreign birth and training.

Kenneth H. Baker, Director of Research of the National Association of Broadcasters, commented, as quoted in *Vocational Opportunities for Foreign Language Students:*

> So far as we are able to discover, the only opportunity for the use of foreign languages in broadcasting would be in the actual reading of scripts in one of the many languages broadcast over standard American radio stations. A list of these languages includes: Italian, Polish, Spanish, German, Czech-Slovak, Portuguese, Lithuanian, Hungarian, Scandinavian, Greek, French, Finnish, Yugoslav, Ukrainian, Chinese, Russian, Japanese, Romanian, Arabic, Dutch, Albanian, Syrian, Latin, Egyptian, Armenian, and Hebrew.
>
> In addition to these languages, the short-wave broadcasts to other countries are also opportunities for the use of foreign languages. In this case, excellence of accent is especially desirable. . . .

David L. Doughty, Assistant to the Manager, National Association of Broadcasters, sees only a limited number of opportunities for the use of foreign languages on domestic radio and TV programs. He wrote:

> Unfortunately, for the individual interested in linguistics as a career combined with broadcasting, there are very few opportunities in American radio and television. In most of the larger cities throughout the country that have good-sized foreign language populations, some stations do special language broadcasts for these groups. However, this is but a fractional segment of the jobs in American broadcasting. Insofar as foreign language students having an interest in broadcasting are concerned, I would say that their best bet would be to contact the Voice of America. . . .

The rapidly increasing exchange of international radio programs has been commented on in connection with the use of radio and television in advertising. Of crucial importance is the use of foreign languages in military intelligence (Foreign Broadcast Intelligence Service and Monitoring Division) and for propaganda purposes (Voice of America). Here a high degree of skill and an impeccable pronunciation are demanded.

International broadcasting has expanded tremendously within the last few years. Arno G. Huth, Consultant to the Pan American Broadcasting Company, wrote in one of its World Wide Special Reports:

Today, international broadcasts, supplemented by the international exchange of television programs, originate in almost every country of the world and reach almost every nation. In the United States alone, no less than six agencies and organizations are engaged in international broadcasting. And like Great Britain and the Soviet Union, which operate the two most important international broadcasting services, Canada, Argentina, France, Italy, Poland, Czechoslovakia, Hungary, Indonesia, India, Pakistan, Australia, and many others are broadcasting day and night in many different languages.

International broadcasting offers great potentialities for worldwide advertising. There are, in various areas of the world, private as well as official stations which accept foreign-sponsored programs and which, although broadcasting mainly in the national language, are prepared to carry foreign-language programs destined to minority groups or to listeners in adjacent countries.

FILM INDUSTRY

There are a number of sections of the motion picture industry in which a knowledge of foreign languages is useful. William Zimmerman, Director, Narrated and Titled Films Department of Metro-Goldwyn-Mayer, wrote:

We employ several young people who have a knowledge of one or more foreign languages. Their knowledge of these languages was a prerequisite of their employment.

The main languages used in this department (the department in this company which has the greatest use for bilingual or multilingual personnel) are Spanish, French, and Portuguese (for Brazil), although we do work in many other languages.

John T. Madden, Personnel Director of the same company, wrote:

We employ persons who are both bilingual and multilingual in the production of films for foreign distribution. As a rule, however, these persons were born in the foreign countries or have a very large background of skill and experience in the language. We also employ translators in the several languages, such as French, German, Spanish, and occasionally other languages.

FOREIGN MISSIONARY WORK

The missionary field engages tens of thousands of persons of all nations. It covers the entire globe and embraces all languages. A knowledge of a foreign language is indispensable to a missionary who wants to be effective. The missionary must not only be able to converse in the tongue of the native but is often called upon to translate technical matter and poetry (hymns) into the foreign language.

In fact, in a number of instances, it was the missionary who gave the language its written form. Bishop Cyril gave the Russians their alphabet; Wulfilas translated the Bible into Gothic and invented the script. In South America, Spanish missionaries and priests constructed grammars and recorded the language of the natives, as in the case of Quechua, the language of the Incas.

One of the largest groups of Protestant missionaries is Wycliffe Bible Translators. They have made the challenge of language translation a central part of their efforts. Missionaries, carefully trained in linguistics, are sent to areas where there is no written language. Through scrupulous, painstaking work, these missionary linguists are able to produce basic readers, and eventually Bible portions, for the people they are serving.

There is a definite trend toward short-term engagements for missionaries, with nearly half serving for between two- and eleven-month periods. The Church of Jesus Christ of Latter-Day Saints (the Mormon church) expects its young members to dedicate two years to missionary service abroad. Before they undertake this task, they are trained in the languages they will be using at the language center at Brigham Young University, Provo, Utah.

HEALTH SERVICES

It is becoming more and more evident to hospital personnel that a knowledge of certain foreign languages is urgently needed in dealing with patients, especially in metropolitan areas where there are many ethnic groups living in the same area. Doctors, nurses, technicians, and social workers find that a knowledge of other languages is very helpful at times.

Doctors have a need for foreign languages in medical school, internships, research, and clinical practice. Specialists in medical research cannot function efficiently without a reading knowledge of Russian, German, or French. Knowledge of a foreign tongue also is essential for American students studying abroad. Thousands of American medical students got their training in medicine at universities in Europe or Latin America. Favorite countries have recently been Italy, Belgium, and Mexico.

In metropolitan areas, doctors daily confront members of minority groups or recent immigrants who cannot describe their symptoms or understand medical instructions in English. Many larger hospitals now hire bilingual personnel and provide instruction in foreign languages to their doctors, nurses, and technicians.

Jerome C. Ford of the Georgetown University School of Languages and Linguistics in Washington, DC, comments: "The need for foreign language speakers in the medical service area, especially of Spanish, is becoming more and more acute."

Skill in a foreign language is useful to anyone engaged in health services—doctors, medical assistants, nurses, dentists, pharmacists, and opticians. A basic knowledge of a foreign language is a necessity for anyone practicing medicine abroad, such as the American medical employees of the disaster relief organization CARE who are working overseas in the developing countries.

INTERNATIONAL RELATIONS

The number of cultural, commercial, and relief associations interested in foreign relations is constantly increasing. On their staffs they need translators, librarians, research workers, representatives, and receptionists. The Institute of International Education has about fifteen persons equipped with foreign languages, including French, German, Spanish, and Portuguese.

On the research staff of the Foreign Policy Association there are a number of persons who know at least one foreign language. The wide expansion of the field of international relations and the large number of

Americans participating in it were stressed in a World Wide Special Report of the Pan American Broadcasting Company:

> Technical assistance operations are undertaken in almost every part of the world. Since the inception of the program (Expanded Program of Technical Assistance of the UN), some 1,600 experts in a wide variety of fields, drawn from 61 different nations, have been employed by the United Nations and its specialized agencies; of these, 956 were in the field, working in underdeveloped countries and territories, at the requests of the governments directly concerned. They surveyed local conditions, provided advice, demonstrated new techniques, set up schools and training centers, and conducted seminars and vocational courses. Simultaneously, under various scholarship and fellowship programs, hundreds of civil servants, technicians, and students from underdeveloped countries are enabled to study abroad modern techniques of public administration, health and welfare services, and agricultural and industrial production.

JOURNALISM

In considering journalism and foreign languages, one thinks of two large areas: the foreign language press of the United States and the foreign departments of English-language newspapers. The former is taken care of largely by natives but, in the second, there are attractive positions for qualified Americans. There is the local staff consisting of newspeople, translators, and the foreign correspondents in various parts of the world. The language facility required is of a high order. L. B. Mickel of the United Press Association commented:

> The United Press application for employment asks: "What languages other than English do you speak and write *fluently?*" We are not interested in those who reply: "Had four years of German" or "can read Spanish," etc.
>
> For instance, we expect an employee on our Paris staff to be able to understand French from an excited native trying to send in a story on the phone. If you can handle news on the phone in a foreign language, you have to be good.
>
> If a man says he can speak Russian, we expect him to understand a Russian broadcast and be able to report it accurately.

H. W. Burch, of the United Press Association, New York, wrote:

Command of at least one foreign language long has been almost a necessity in the world press association field for any aspiring journalist, since so great a part of news gathering and distribution passes beyond local or national boundaries. The importance, therefore, of foreign language study for anyone hoping to enter world journalism is plain.

The expansion of world communications also has brought new emphasis to the need for foreign language study. This applies in many ways: the great increase in world travel has brought many more foreign students and journalists into contact with each other, forcing them to increase their language facility; a vast increase in the volume of news which can be delivered to remote points by modern radio channels has brought all public information media into closer, speedier contact; the pressures of hot and cold wars, and the dislocations accompanying them have forced interchanges between populations, and accompanying exchange of language habits.

As distribution of news abroad increases with the aid of new radio and telegraphic communications devices, demand increases for editorial workers capable of handling one or more languages. The United Press now transmits its entire news report to Latin America in Spanish, with a full translation-editorial staff employed in New York solely for the purpose of writing the service in Spanish.

It also is worth noting that as the United States has assumed leadership in so many fields of world activity, New York and Washington have become the headquarters for many offices and directive bureaus employing translators, interviewers, commentators, and executives with a command of languages.

There are, in fact, so many visible opportunities for the bilingual or trilingual person that no persuasion should be needed for the aspiring student or adult to perfect herself or himself in a foreign language.

LIBRARY SCIENCE

Knowledge of a foreign language is an important asset to a librarian, especially in the cataloging and reference departments.

Helen R. Sattley, Director, School Library Service, New York, said:

There are indeed many opportunities open in the library field for young people who are adequately trained in one or more foreign languages. All of our library schools require that students present a background in foreign language study for admittance.

Concerning the opportunities for work in library fields for those with a foreign language background, there is much to be said at the present time. For example, all of our large city libraries have foreign book collections. Some of these cities have special branches which concentrate on specific foreign language books. Also, large and important technical and science libraries and departments of science and technology in large libraries need librarians who can read the technical German and French reference books, journals, and magazines. This field is an expanding one at the present time and there is a need for many young men and women who are specifically trained for these positions.

There have been openings in library service outside of the United States; for instance, the information libraries of the United States Department of State have been developed in many important cities throughout the world. It is usual in these libraries for the librarian to meet a foreign language requirement for the country in which the library is located.

There are also permanent libraries in foreign countries, such as the American Library in Paris and the Benjamin Franklin Library in Mexico City. Librarians in these need to have excellent backgrounds in French and Spanish, respectively. There are at the present time and will be in the future, many opportunities for exchange positions among American librarians and those of other countries. A foreign language background will be a necessary requirement. . . .

Faye Simkin, Executive Officer of the New York Public Library, wrote:

The Research Libraries have three major language divisions—the Jewish, Oriental, and Slavonic Division. In addition, the General Research and Humanities Division houses material in most other foreign languages as do our subject divisions. Some 3,000 languages are represented in the collections by language. Among current acquisitions, 50 percent have been ordered in a language other than English.

A knowledge of foreign languages is, of course, a great asset in working in the Research Libraries. However, it is equally as important to have subject skills and to possess the ability to work well in the area of human relationships, both with fellow staff members and the general public.

The New York Public Library, in addition to its vast central reference collection, maintains circulating collections in twenty-two foreign languages. These are: Chinese, Croatian, Czech, Danish, Dutch, Finnish, French (9 branches), German (8), Greek, Hebrew (3), Hungarian (3), Italian (5), Lithuanian, Norwegian, Polish, Portuguese, Russian, Slovak, Spanish (4), Swedish, Ukrainian, and Yiddish (4).

MUSEUM WORK

As in every field of research, in museum work there is need for a knowledge of foreign languages. John R. Saunders, Chair of the Department of Public Instruction of the American Museum of Natural History, New York, said:

> I should say that in any large museum, whether it be devoted to art, science, or history, a command of one or more foreign languages would be a definite asset to a staff member. Most museums cannot afford to employ translators regularly. They usually depend upon the linguistic ability of their regular staff. Most of our staff who are concerned with research have at least a reading knowledge of French and German. Several are adept in Spanish. Those who do their field work in Mexico, Central America, and South America find it necessary to learn to speak and understand Spanish. When a translation problem comes up at the Museum, resources are pooled, and since we make a language ability survey every so often, there is usually someone on hand who can assist in the matter.

PUBLISHING

There are some forty important publishers of foreign language books in the United States. Dr. Vincenzo Cioffari, formerly the Modern Language Editor of D. C. Heath & Company, commented:

> Whereas a few years ago the publishing industry dealt almost exclusively with printed textbooks, now it has to deal with complete programs which include tapes, charts, television courses, programmed courses, and other materials. Consequently there has been an increase not only in the

actual editorial staffs, but in supplementary staffs which deal with laboratories, audio-visual materials, television programs, etc.

On the whole, publishing houses have an editorial staff composed of people who are quite familiar with two, three, or four modern foreign languages. These staffs are responsible for the correctness of the foreign language that gets into print. When necessary, these staffs are expanded by the use of part-time, trained editors who work at home.

In addition to the actual editorial staff, there is a staff of proofreaders maintained by the press rather than the publisher. There is a staff of trained technicians maintained by recording studios dealing with tapes, or television programs. All of these people must be familiar with foreign languages; the more languages they have at their command, the more valuable they are.

SECRETARIAL WORK

One of the most attractive positions in business for a beginner, and possibly one of the easiest for which to qualify, is that of bilingual stenographer, secretary, or administrative assistant. These positions are on different levels, depending upon the size and character of the business and on the preparation of the applicant.

Although this type of job is usually associated with typing and stenography—the basic skills of the secretary—the duties may go far beyond that. The office assistant may be a typist, a stenographer, a receptionist, a file clerk, or the chief executive's managerial assistant. The latter position of trust and importance is usually attained only after some years of experience and skill development.

SOCIAL WORK

Social workers in metropolitan areas deal every day with members of minority groups, and without some knowledge of a foreign language, they cannot work effectively. This is evident in the want-ads for social workers, many of which ask for competency in Spanish. Some of the larger social service agencies like Cancer Care and Travelers Air International Social Service of America, now require their workers to have a knowledge of Spanish, Italian, Chinese, modern Greek, Korean, Vietnamese, Thai, and Russian, and other languages are also useful, of course, depending upon the ethnic group with whom the social worker is dealing.

Other organizations like the Salvation Army, the Volunteers of America, the Red Cross, and the YMCA have also urged some of their employees to develop competence in a foreign language for use in their social-service work.

Professor Arthur Dunham of the School of Social Work of the University of Michigan said:

> In at least a minority of positions in social work, knowledge of certain foreign languages would be of real practical value. These positions would include such jobs as the following: (1) social work in foreign countries; (2) social work with certain American agencies working primarily with the foreign born, such as the International Institutes, organizations working with displaced persons; (3) social work in certain districts of larger cities.

TRANSLATION

In its broadest sense, as applied to language, translation is the act or process of expressing an idea or message in some target language other than the source language in which it is given to the translator. Translation of the spoken language is called "interpretation," and the term "translation" is reserved primarily for written or printed material. The distinction is important because the two activities make use of quite different linguistic skills. Translators need have little facility in the spoken language since their work does not require it. Consequently they tend to avoid acting as interpreters, although some are called upon for that purpose occasionally.

There is a wide demand for translators in business, in various research organizations, and in government service. The New York City telephone directory lists a large number of translation bureaus.

Those who go into this field must be prepared to deal with all kinds of scientific, technical, commercial, and legal material. Many translators work freelance. The director of the Engineering Societies Library said:

> We do not employ full-time translators, but use part-time help. Most of our translation is from German to English or from French to English, but during the past year we have translated Italian, Japanese, Hungarian, Russian, Spanish and probably other languages. The rate of payment depends on the difficulty of the work and the language.

The three main categories of materials that are most frequently translated are commercial, literary, and technical. The first category includes letters, contracts, and advertisements; the second consists of novels, poems, and historical articles; the technical category comprises material for various sciences and engineering.

The translator must be familiar not only with both languages but should also have some knowledge of the subject covered in the text. This frequently entails extensive research and the use of special technical dictionaries.

A translation can be considered successful only if it achieves its purpose. A good literary translation should convey the emotional and artistic as well as the informational content of the original. The language should be completely normal and natural, so that the reader is almost unaware that he or she is dealing with a translation.

To qualify as an efficient translator, a person should have a well-rounded college education. In addition to the language course, the aspirant should cover many special areas such as science, history, law, economics, and literature.

The constant growth in the number of United States patents issued to residents of other countries has created an increasing need for technical translators. The expansion of American business all over the world has raised the demand for translators of correspondence, advertising, and technical matter.

Machine translation of texts has been a goal since computers first came on the scene. Unfortunately, to translate natural language with 100 percent accuracy is at present beyond the scope of computer programming because the task requires more than factual knowledge about a language. It also requires much knowledge of the world, adaptation and meaning to different contexts, some common sense correction, and a perception of the idiosyncracies of idiom and metaphor. At present, *machine-assisted* translation is the most that can be expected. Many texts have to be pre-edited to help the computer in its task, and practically all require post-editing to ensure that the result is accurate and readable.

Machine translation of routine documents written in agreed-upon formulations and straightforward technical reports is now possible, as well as preliminary translation that copes with the more obvious transpositions, thus reducing the time the translator must spend on the text. Research is continuing. Would-be translators should keep a close eye on development in this field.

A growing number of American industries maintain language staffs of one or more translators, including Rockwell International, Otis Engineering, Honeywell, and Kodak. Salaries are somewhat higher than those offered by international agencies, but the translator in private industry is usually required to have competence in a number of languages—five or more—and to act as escort interpreter for visitors, as well as answering telephone calls.

The number of positions in which translating alone is required are not very numerous. In business the practice is to hire someone proficient in one or more languages who also possesses a technical skill such as banking, marketing, or foreign trade.

Translators and interpreters are employed in various departments of the federal government and the United Nations. There are also positions available in publishing houses and firms doing business with foreign countries.

Salaries depend not only on linguistic proficiency but also on the degree of technical skill in some other area. In the federal government, translators with a BA degree are given GS-5 ratings (depending on college grades). Beginning salaries in 1997 in these grades were $19,520 for GS-5 and approximately $24,178 for GS-7 (see also Chapter 6).

Although there are many staff translators, the majority are freelance and work as they are needed. They are generally paid a set fee per typed page.

The largest single producer of translations among the government agencies is the Joint Publications Research Service (JPRS), an agency of the Central Intelligence Agency. Most of the translating is done by freelance translators instead of private translation services. The bulk of JPRS translation work in the past has been from Soviet and East European publications.

Translation is a very important and interesting activity. The daily production will vary with the difficulty of the text. Most translators are expected to complete between 2,000 and 4,000 words per day of finished typed translations, but some experienced translators who dictate are capable of translating more than 20,000 words per day. "Translator Training Guidelines" and a list of schools offering training for translators and interpreters are available from the American Translators Association, 109 Croton Avenue, Ossining, NY 10562. Valuable information also may be secured from the Language Service Division, U. S. Department of State, Washington, DC 20520.

TRAVEL AND TOURISM

Although there has been a recent decline due to international exchange factors, travel and tourism is still big business in the United States. Millions of tourists visit our country each year. Yet, strangely enough, the need for a foreign language background is not as urgent in the travel agency field as one might expect. W. F. McGrath, Executive Vice-President of the American Society of Travel Agents, wrote:

> There is no way of knowing to what extent the use of foreign languages would be used in the travel field, as this would depend on the type of business only. By and large, travel agents in this country utilize the services of corresponding firms in foreign countries for most services and do not have to be linguists. In addition, the use of the English language is universal in the travel industry.

Although great pains have been taken to provide comfortable hotel accommodations and travel facilities, the language barrier still remains a problem. Many foreign visitors suffer more than a little inconvenience because most Americans can converse in no language other than English. Some efforts have been made to remedy this fault by employing multilingual travel personnel.

Concerning foreign language usage in various lodging facilities, Mr. Mel Sandler, Employee Relations Consultant for the American Hotel and Motel Association stated the following:

> Language capability is an asset for employees both in terms of guest contact and services, but also to converse with hotel staff who often have better command of languages other than English. Degree of need for language resources may vary with location and clientele.

Employees of the Waldorf-Astoria in New York represent a number of different languages. The personnel director wrote:

> We have a large number of guests from abroad, and to take care of the situation where languages are involved, we have a Foreign Department, the head of which speaks approximately eight languages fluently. We also have in that department an assistant who speaks Spanish and Portuguese fluently and several other employees, such as stenographers, typists, etc., who are linguists. I think that the knowledge of a foreign language, or several languages, is an aid in securing employment in any large hotel where they would be likely to have clientele from abroad.

In a recent survey sponsored by the Department of Recreation, Parks and Tourism at Clemson University, questionnaires were sent to numerous tour operators in West Germany, France, Spain, and Japan. One of the clearly perceived needs that should be filled is that of more tours and travel literature in the major languages. There is some evidence that initiatives are being undertaken in the United States to make greater use of foreign languages with these millions of visitors. But much more needs to be done. It would seem a very promising market for enterprising linguists who like to work with the public.

CHAPTER 8

TEACHING LANGUAGES

Those seriously contemplating foreign language teaching as a career may be interested in some historical background on their chosen vocation. After this short survey, we will discuss the current situation in the United States and how languages are taught in the schools and universities, with some information on the supporting role of the U.S. government as it endeavors to encourage and promote foreign languages and international studies.

HISTORICAL BACKGROUND

During the Middle Ages, Latin was the universal language of the cultured, at least as far as Western Europe was concerned. It was the official language of the church and universities. Lectures and discussions were conducted in that tongue. All state documents and scientific treatises were written in Latin. The first printed book, the Gutenberg Bible, appeared in Latin. Since this language was indispensable for any higher education, it was the mainstay of school instruction, especially on the secondary level.

From the time of the disintegration of the Roman Empire, however, the popular Latin spoken in the marketplace and in military camps gradually assumed new aspects. Endings were dropped, case forms were simplified, and pronunciation was changed. In the former provinces of the Empire, new national languages developed—French, Spanish, Italian,

Portuguese, Catalan, and Romanian—called collectively the "Romance" languages. The language of Germany was not deeply affected by Latin since only the Rhine had been occupied by the Romans. In Great Britain, English developed out of the Anglo-Saxon of the Germanic invaders, the Latin of the church, and the French of the Norman conquerors in the eleventh century.

These national languages continued to develop and to assert themselves. Distinguished writers such as Dante, Petrarch, and Chaucer began to use the vernacular for prose and poetry. Latin was gradually dropped as a medium of literary expression. The wider employment of the vernacular as a medium of instruction in the schools received great impetus from the Reformation, which stressed the reading of the Bible in the language of common people.

Slowly but surely everyday speech also invaded the universities and other seats of learning. As early as the beginning of the sixteenth century, Paracelsus, the noted physician and philosopher, attacked the use of Latin and the barren learning of the scholars and proceeded to give his lectures in German. In France, the famous essayist, Montaigne records that in 1539, at the age of six, he was sent to the distinguished college of Guyenne, where Latin was no longer used in teaching.

It was not, however, until the middle of the eighteenth century that Latin was displaced as the standard language in higher institutions of learning. A leader in bringing this about was the philosopher and mathematician Leibniz, who stressed the importance of modern languages.

Succeeding the classical languages of Latin and Greek in the curriculum of the secondary schools and partly displacing them, the modern languages took over, in large part, the traditional grammar method employed in teaching the ancient tongues. Students did not learn to speak the new languages, but to read, translate, and grammatically analyze texts. Gradually languages became essentially school subjects, taught for their educational and cultural values as an introduction to literary studies.

Intelligent people realized very soon that dealing with a living language in this manner was ineffective. One of the most significant comments is that of the Moravian educator Comenius, who says in his *Magna Didacta* (1632): "Every language must be learned by practice rather than by rules, especially by reading, repeating, copying, and by written and oral attempts at imitation."

This important basic principle, however, was ignored. It was not until the nineteenth century, with increased interest in sound systems and opportunities for travel, that language experts became interested in more effective methods of learning foreign languages for oral communication. They began to stress the need to introduce the student to the language in its spoken form from the beginning. Some reformers developed a so-called natural method. Among these was a German, Gottlieb Heness, and a Frenchman, Sauveur, who started a private language school in 1866 in New Haven, Connecticut. These teachers established the first summer language school with short, intensive courses.

Claude Marcel, who published a significant treatise on language teaching in 1867, stood for the dictum: "Learn to read by reading." He wanted students to "think" in the language and read without translating or resorting to dictionary use. Students then discussed in the language what they had read. Marcel exerted considerable influence on language teaching, especially in the United States.

In the New World, there was a great interest in various foreign languages from the earliest times. New England, particularly, was favored with persons of a scholarly bent, and the libraries of clergymen, doctors, and lawyers frequently contained books in French, German, Italian, Spanish, and Latin. Many of the more educated people took private lessons from native tutors.

Benjamin Franklin was an ardent student of foreign languages and did much to promote their instruction. In his *Autobiography,* he tells how he progressed in his linguistic pursuits: "I had begun in 1733 to study languages; I soon made myself so much a Master of the French as to be able to read the books with ease. I then undertook the Italian." Practical minded as he was, he recommended Latin, Greek, and French for students of medicine; Latin and French for law students; and French, German, and Spanish for those entering the business world.

Henry Wadsworth Longfellow was the first Professor of Modern Languages at Bowdoin College in 1829 and later at Harvard. He taught French, German, Italian, Spanish, and wrote grammar texts, readers, and exercise manuals.

German

During the nineteenth century, German was taught extensively in many private and public schools. Throughout the United States, many day schools were founded by German-Americans who wanted the language transmitted to their children. The extent and influence of these German schools was amazing. They became so numerous that a school law enacted in Pennsylvania placed them on a par with the English schools. In Ohio, the 1840 legislature directed all boards of education to introduce German wherever it was requested by seven citizens.

In the early 1900s, German was taught in the elementary schools of St. Louis, Baltimore, Cleveland, Chicago, Dayton, Denver, Buffalo, Milwaukee, St. Paul, San Francisco, and New York. As late as 1914, one-third of the entire elementary school population of Cincinnati was learning German.

German enjoyed this favorable position until the entry of the United States into World War I. At that time, enrollments dropped drastically, and only a little more than one-half of one percent of the total high school population was enrolled in German. After the war, however, the language experienced a rapid recovery and returned to its former popularity. A further decline occurred after World War II.

A loss of enrollments in German was registered by the Modern Language Association in the 1970s and early 1980s; this seems now to have changed, with interest in languages again on the rise. German remains third in popularity in schools and colleges. Predictions are that German will regain its importance in international affairs, trade, and commerce with the changing face of Europe and its own strong position in science and technology, particularly engineering.

French

French has been widely taught at all levels in the United States over the centuries. It has always been regarded as a prestige language because of France's outstanding writers, artists, and philosophers, and the wide use of French as a diplomatic language. It is still used as a second language in many parts of Africa and Asia; it is a preferred foreign language in some parts of the Middle East, Latin America, and Europe; and it is one of the major languages for use in international agencies. The number of people in the United States who speak French as a native language is small compared with Spanish, but there are significant French-speaking populations in Louisiana (Cajuns) and in parts of New England; these are descendants of the Acadians who left Quebec after its incorporation into predominantly English-speaking Canada. In a number of areas there are Haitian populations who speak French or Haitian Creole, derived from French. There are French-speaking areas close to the United States not only in Quebec Province, but also in Martinique and Guadeloupe in the Caribbean. French enjoys second position after Spanish in total language enrollments in the United States. From 1986–1990, however, it suffered a slight decline in enrollments, whereas Spanish registered a 30 percent gain, now enrolling twice as many students as are enrolled in French (which enrolls twice as many as the third place language, German).

Italian

With the immigration of millions of Italians to the United States, this language has always attracted a number of students. In 1995, with 43,800 students, it had the fourth highest enrollment, although it had less than a tenth of the number of students learning Spanish. Even though Italian was offered at colleges and universities, it did not enter public school curricula until 1922, when it was placed on a par with other languages in New York City. It is still stronger at the college level. Many students of Italian family origin are attracted to the language of their ancestors. It has become a popular second foreign language with others and has considerable interest for music, art, and architecture students.

Spanish

Spanish, like Italian, historically had many ardent devotees. During the nineteenth century, however, it seldom appeared in the curricula of schools and colleges. Only in some elementary schools of New Mexico was it a subject of instruction. The War with Mexico (1846–1848) stimulated a short-lived interest in the language; however, the greatest boon to Spanish came with the outbreak of World War I. Enrollments rose from 36,000 in 1915 to 252,000 in 1922. One of the great public incentives to study Spanish was the popular notion that increased trade with Latin America would provide many new and lucrative positions for young Americans.

The large influx of Puerto Ricans, Cubans, and Mexicans into the United States in the last few decades also has given a strong boost to Spanish enrollments. Americans also have become much more aware of the fact that there are large concentrations of Spanish speakers in the southwest regions of the United States, particularly in California, New Mexico, and Texas. Over the last decade, the number of students learning Spanish has more than doubled in the high schools. Spanish now has the highest enrollment figures among modern languages at all levels of instruction, above all others in the following survey.

Higher Education Registrations in Foreign Languages: 1970 to 1995

					[As of fall]				
ITEM	**1970**	**1972**	**1974**	**1977**	**1980**	**1983**	**1986**	**1990**	**1995**
Registrations[1] (1,000)	**1,111.5**	**1,008.9**	**946.6**	**933.5**	**924.8**	**966.0**	**1,003.2**	**1,184.1**	**1,138.8**
Index (1960 = 100)	171.8	155.9	146.3	144.3	142.9	149.3	155.0	183.0	176.0
By selected language (1,000):									
Spanish	389.2	364.5	362.2	376.7	379.4	386.2	411.3	533.9	606.3
French	359.3	293.1	253.1	246.1	248.4	270.1	275.3	272.5	205.4
German	202.6	177.1	152.1	135.4	126.9	128.2	121.0	133.3	96.3
Italian	34.2	33.3	33.0	33.3	34.8	38.7	40.9	49.7	43.8
Japanese	6.6	8.3	9.6	10.7	11.5	16.1	23.5	45.7	44.7
Russian	36.1	36.4	32.5	27.8	24.0	30.4	34.0	44.6	24.7
Latin	27.6	24.4	25.2	24.4	25.0	24.2	25.0	28.2	25.9
Chinese	6.2	10.0	10.6	9.8	11.4	13.2	16.9	19.5	26.5
Ancient Greek	16.7	20.6	24.4	25.8	22.1	19.4	17.6	16.4	16.3
Hebrew	16.6	21.1	22.4	19.4	19.4	18.2	15.6	13.0	13.1
Portuguese	5.1	4.8	5.1	5.0	4.9	4.4	5.1	6.2	6.5
Arabic	1.3	1.7	2.0	3.1	3.5	3.4	3.4	3.5	4.4
12 languages as percent of total	99.1	98.7	98.5	98.3	98.5	98.6	98.6	98.5	97.8

[1] Includes other foreign languages, not shown separately.

Source: Association of Departments of Foreign Languages, New York, NY, *ADFL Bulletin*, vol. 28, No. 2, and earlier issues (copyright). Reprinted in *Statistical Abstracts of the United States* (1997).

CURRENT SITUATION IN THE UNITED STATES

There has been a toughening of standards for incoming foreign language teachers. The level of competence in the language is now expected to be high, and a period of residence or study in a target language country rapidly improves control of the language. Increasingly there is a call for oral proficiency testing of graduates.

Foreign language teachers are also expected to understand the processes of language learning and to have studied the linguistics and associated culture of the language they teach. They are required to take a course in techniques of teaching languages and testing student achievement; this is usually accompanied by a period of practice or student teaching, which candidates will be expected to have taken. (It is essential before completing training to check the specific requirements for state certification in the states in which you prefer to teach.)

With the growing demand for courses that are more practical in nature than literary, candidate teachers will make themselves more attractive if they can offer such courses as French, Spanish, or German for business, or Spanish for health professionals or law enforcement. They will be expected to be familiar enough with the culture of the various countries speaking the language to be able to supplement textbooks with materials they have personally acquired, such as newspaper and magazine articles, menus, air and train schedules, or posters. They should also know where to find suitable poems and short stories from various target-language areas to enliven and broaden the scope of what may be a fairly routine, though solidly structured textbook, selected without consultation by the department head. It is also currently presumed that candidates will be familiar with suitable videos and films, and available material for the language laboratory and computer-assisted language learning. If they are ready and willing to organize exchange programs for their students in a country where the language is spoken, this will often also be a plus. Much information on these matters is available at the meetings and in the publications of the various language associations listed in Appendix A.

In order to broaden what they can offer to an employing school, it is advisable for prospective teachers to be certified in two languages if possible, or in one language and another subject area, particularly if the language offered is not one that normally has high enrollments.

If the applicant is agreeable to a position in a small town or rural community, the likelihood of being placed will be brighter in a period of diminishing demand. Although the public schools in general pay better, the atmosphere and working conditions in many private and parochial schools are more attractive to some and may make up for the lower pay.

As in other fields, there has been a marked increase in teachers' salaries in recent years. In 1995, the average annual salary for secondary school teachers in public schools was $35,500 (compared to $33,400 for elementary school teachers and $32,300 for special education teachers, according to the *Occupational Outlook Quarterly,* spring 1997).

An exciting teaching opportunity for young American teachers that deserves mention is teaching in overseas dependents schools. Such positions are available to most certified teachers and can be especially interesting for language teachers, if the school is in a country where a language they have studied is spoken. For current requirements, contact the Department of Defense, Office of Dependents Schools, 2461 Eisenhower Avenue, Alexandria, VA 22331. Other overseas opportunities sometimes arise in American Schools abroad and in International School Services, 15 Roszel Road, P.O. Box 5910, Princeton, NJ 08543.

When setting your sights on teaching overseas, remember that the popularity of particular foreign languages and opportunities to teach them vary according to geographic, economic, and political factors. This regional variability will affect the employment possibilities for the particular language you offer. In many places, native speakers of a specific language are available locally, and these teachers are usually given preference.

In Canada, for instance, because of the official aim of creating a bilingual country, French as a second language is the major educational thrust among English speakers, and there are many core French programs in the schools, as well as the popular French immersion programs. However, native-speaking teachers from within Canada are given preference to ensure a Canadian flavor to the teaching. To work in Canada, one must usually be a landed immigrant, if one is not a Canadian citizen. According to the American Forum for Education in Global and International Studies, in the United Kingdom, which is just across the channel from the European continent and is committed to becoming an integral part of Europe, 84 percent of student language enrollments are in French, 55 percent in German, 29 percent in Spanish and Portuguese, 15 percent in Italian, 10 percent in Russian, and 2 percent in Dutch, but native speakers of these languages are close at hand in other parts of Europe.

Private commercial language schools and federal language schools in this country usually employ native speakers as teachers. The positions are frequently part-time, and employment fluctuates with the demand. Most private language schools keep rosters of available part-time teachers in specific languages, upon whom they call when a need arises. English speakers often enjoy teaching English to speakers of other languages (TESOL) in private language schools abroad, and the demand for English is increasing rapidly at the present time throughout the world. Before taking up such positions, however, it is important to obtain some language teaching training to avoid the awkward situation of having to muddle through in what is a very demanding undertaking.

FOREIGN LANGUAGE TEACHING IN THE UNITED STATES

For decades, the study of foreign languages was neglected in the United States because, unlike the situation in many countries around the world, there was no economic or social pressure to learn other tongues. In American schools, study of a second language has usually been on an elective basis, whereas in Europe, it has been a required subject, considered sufficiently important for students to devote many years to its study. When World War II erupted, the U.S. Department of Defense found that very few of its military personnel were able to communicate in another language, even one they had studied in school. As for Japanese, a knowledge of which was extremely important, only about 15 percent of the 200,000 enlistees and officers in the navy possessed a working competence in that language.

Because of the urgent need for interpreters, the Army Specialized Training Program (ASTP) was set up to provide immediate instruction in some fifty foreign languages. With intensive teaching methods in small groups, each with the assistance of a "native informant," many contact hours, the use of records and films, and a clearly focused goal (ability to communicate in everyday language on military subjects in order to interrogate prisoners), selected students with high motivation made very rapid progress in a relatively short period of time.

The ASTP methods were later tried out and refined in a few universities and schools and evolved into the aural-oral or audiolingual method of teaching languages. This approach was noted for its emphasis on students listening to spoken language at a normal rate of delivery from the beginning; the memorizing of dialogues of authentic informal speech that students then tried to vary and use in situational role-playing in class; saturation drills with immediate feedback on correctness of response (this practice being reinforced with individual work in the language laboratory); and a minimum of grammatical explanation so that students would be encouraged to learn how the language worked by observation, attempting to develop their own utterances by analogy with what they had heard. In class, students were given opportunities to practice correct utterances by the device of choral response. Reading and writing were delayed until the students had a good command of the spoken language, except where graphic representation of the language helped to consolidate the oral learning.

The launching of *Sputnik* by the Soviet Union in 1957 had a startling impact on the Western world, as people became aware that the Soviets had made great strides in scientific and technological research without the rest of the world being aware of it. It soon became apparent that, had Americans been able to read Russian, they would have known of these advances much earlier through the scientific literature. Specialists began to study the Soviet educational system and drew attention to the fact that their teaching of science and mathematics (and foreign languages) was clearly superior to that in the United States. Federal authorities realized that training in science, mathematics, and foreign languages was not merely a matter of vocational preparation, but also a vital function of national defense. In view of this, the National Defense Education Act (NDEA) was passed, allotting millions of dollars to provide stronger teaching in these three areas. Under the NDEA, thousands of teachers were trained in the audiolingual method at summer institutes in colleges and universities across the country.

The United States Department of Education, through its Center for International Education (CIE) administers a variety of activities to expand international and global knowledge in the United States. CIE activities include foreign language and area training, curriculum development, and research, as well as support for dissertation and faculty research abroad and special group projects and seminars overseas. In a revival of attention to foreign languages, in 1990, the Department of Education funded three National Foreign Language Research Centers (NFLRCs). The first, at the Second Language Teaching and Curriculum Center at the University of Hawaii at Manoa, supported a fellowship program to bring internationally known professors to the Center to conduct research and also internships for teachers of Indo-Pacific languages; the second, at the Language Acquisition Research Center at San Diego State University, concentrated on foreign language acquisition research and the training of teachers in improved methods of teaching languages and efficient and innovative use of technology; the third, at Georgetown University and the Center for Applied Linguistics (CAL), conducted research into language learning, teaching, and testing, to train teachers through workshops, expand the database for the Survey of Materials for the Study of the Less Commonly Taught Languages, and maintain CAL's Educational Research Information Clearinghouse (ERIC).

In 1991, Congress passed the National Security Education Act (NSEA) establishing an international education trust fund of $150 million, the income from which will be used to finance scholarships for undergraduates to study overseas, curriculum grants to colleges and universities for programs in international and area studies and foreign languages, and fellowships for graduate students in those fields. Foreign languages are once again being recognized as of national importance.

Much time has passed since the heyday of the audiolingual method, which was criticized for being too centered on automatic control of discrete grammatical structures. In the 1970s, emphasis in the field turned to the importance of developing what was called communicative competence, which went far beyond the manipulation of grammatical structures to include pragmatic and strategic competence (that is, the ability to use the language appropriately with correct discourse features in the context of another culture). Following the lead of the Council of Europe, language specialists began to research the functions language utterances express, and the circumstances in which foreign language users will be expected to communicate, with the intention of developing some congruence between the two in teaching materials and classwork. There was, and continues to be, great emphasis on the importance of understanding another culture in order to be able to operate within it.

To summarize, this is a period of diversity in foreign language teaching, where courses are developed to meet many objectives—practical, cultural, literary, or career-oriented. There is a strong emphasis on spoken communicative ability. Whether one begins with extensive listening or combines listening and speaking from the beginning, the objective now is reception and production of meaningful and culturally appropriate discourse in normal contexts of language use. There is growing stress on comprehending and interpreting written texts in culturally authentic ways, while producing texts oneself that reflect the discourse structure and semantic interrelationships of the new language. At all levels, students are expected to demonstrate a usable control of language for the purposes for which the course was designed.

Pedagogically, there is a focus on learning through student-directed and maintained tasks, cooperatively performed, often in small groups; in other words, the student is considered an active language learner rather than the passive recipient of the wisdom of others. With this emphasis on the language learner, there is much interest in individual learning strategies. Many methodologists now believe that language is learned more efficiently if there is less emphasis on form and more on function (that is, using the language from the early stages to express meanings of interest to the students in the kinds of circumstances in which they may later need to use the language, whether oral or written form). Dramatic activity, particularly original skits prepared by groups of students, has been found to be a useful format within which students can express their own meanings; these are frequently videotaped for later analysis and critique.

Since individual control of language for whatever purpose is now central, more attention is being paid to materials for advanced learners, a group whose needs have often been overlooked in the recent past. Americans are finally recognizing the fact that successful language learning takes time. At the intermediate and advanced levels, there is much experimentation with content-based instruction (that is, developing and perfecting the students' competence in the language while they are concentrating on subject matter taught in that language). This trend has given foreign languages a more interdisciplinary role, as students study such subjects as economics, history, international relations, art appreciation, or film in Spanish, or German, or French. At lower levels, this approach has found expression in the development of immersion programs.

Finally, innovative programs are being developed for computer-assisted language learning, with a listening component, often incorporating visual materials from the target country on videodisc. Authentic programs are being taken from satellite emissions from target-language countries for use in class; film and video are well-established course materials, often with students videotaping their own productions; and technology enables students to communicate directly with their counterparts who speak the target language. Distance learning via satellite-distributed television, with individual telephone interviews with native speakers as follow-up, is bringing high-quality language teaching to the smallest and most isolated schools. Whatever the form of the program, teachers are now concerned that their students be able to demonstrate some level of proficiency after they complete their course, in the sense that they can actually do something with the language material they have acquired. Testing reflects this pragmatic approach and seeks to set the students real tasks, rather than emphasizing the accumulation of separate bits of knowledge. Language is finally being viewed as an integrated whole that can be a purposeful and enjoyable addition to the students' life skills.

BILINGUAL EDUCATION AND TESOL

The United States is predominantly an English-speaking country, although large numbers of its people speak languages other than English.

From 1821 until 1981, more than fifty million immigrants of extremely varied ethnic origin have come to its shores. According to the most recent U.S. census, the six foreign languages most often spoken at home were Spanish, Italian, German, French, Polish, and Chinese.

From this list, it is evident that the foreign languages most widely spoken in the United States are Spanish, Italian, German, and French. There are, however, many other languages spoken in various parts of the United States, especially in metropolitan areas. In New York City, for example, large numbers of people speak Chinese, Japanese, Portuguese, Greek, Haitian Creole, Lithuanian, Russian, Hungarian, Danish, Swedish, Norwegian, Albanian, and Yiddish, among others.

The United States has always been a country of immigrants, who have had to acquire the dominant language, English, in order to advance and become a full part of the larger society. From the early days of U.S. history, there have been concentrations of people speaking the same language who have taken measures to ensure the maintenance of their language and culture and to ensure that their children received a solid education while acquiring enough English to continue in that language. This was noticeably the case with German immigrants in the Milwaukee and Cincinnati areas, where bilingual education, using German and English, was set up to draw German-speaking children into the public schools, where they would mix with English-speaking children. Bilingual education programs also existed on Indian reservations. Unfortunately, there is also a long history of groups of lower socioeconomic standing being submersed in English education, who have dropped out of school early because of humiliation, frustration, or lack of success.

The widespread development of bilingual education sprang out of the demands for equality of opportunity of the civil rights movement of the 1960s. Already in the 1960s, with large influxes of Cubans into the Miami area, experiments with bilingual education had taken place with considerable success in Dade County, Florida. These bilingual classes were enrichment classes in which the children of educated Cubans and middle-class English speakers learned together in the two languages, Spanish and English.

In 1968, the Bilingual Education Act (Title VII) was passed to meet the demands of Mexican Americans in the Southwest for equal educational opportunities to stem the flood of dropouts among their children. The act was designed to recognize the special educational needs of limited English proficient (LEP) students from low-income families and to stimulate innovative programs that would eventually be taken over and supported by the states. Bilingual education programs received a major impetus from the *Lau v. Nicholls* case, which was argued before the Supreme Court in 1974 (Chinese public school students versus the San Francisco Unified School District). As a result of this supporting decision, bilingual programs were established in the district for Chinese, Filipinos, and Spanish-speakers, with English as a Second Language (ESL) classes for others. This led to an amendment to the Bilingual Education Act, broadening eligibility by removing income restrictions. In accordance with the "Lau remedies," LEPs were to be identified and instructed in their dominant language until they were sufficiently advanced in English to be mainstreamed into regular English medium classes—that is, a system of transitional bilingual education. During the 1970s, many states mandated such transitional bilingual programs in areas where there were concentrations of children speaking a language other than English. In 1978, there was a great expansion of federal subsidies to include teacher training programs and resource centers. Gradually the area of bilingual education has moved into the state domain with the reduction of federal funds.

There is still much controversy about bilingual education. Some feel that English is the language of the United States and that its status is threatened by bilingual education. Much of the controversy is based on misconceptions, that there is an enormous amount of bilingual education and that the programs are maintenance programs that impede the learning of English by children who speak other languages. Not all non-English-speaking children, by any means, are out of mainstream classes. And the laws of the states mandate that the bilingual programs be transitional, to facilitate the passage of LEPs into completely English education. Many LEPs receive ESL instruction in the mainstream schools, where they are out of their mainstream classes at certain times to receive special instruction to improve their English skills. Hence, there is a need for both bilingual teachers and ESL teachers in the schools.

Since much of LEP instructions is at the elementary level, bilingual teachers and ESL teachers interested in teaching at the lower level should be fully trained elementary schoolteachers. In most states they need special certification. Bilingual teachers must, of course, be fully proficient in the dominant language of their students and able to teach content areas in that language, while increasing the English skills of their students, with the aim of eventually mainstreaming them successfully (usually at about the fourth-grade level). They also should be familiar with the culture of their students, their ways of learning and interacting, and their value systems. Larger universities and many colleges have bilingual education programs to prepare bilingual teachers for certification.

ESL students speak so many different languages that their teachers cannot hope to learn them all. Teachers should have specialized training in ESL. Having learned another language themselves will make them more sensitive to the problems of their students and to cultural differences. Some ESL teachers teach only a few ESL classes as part of their scheduled load, so they need to be trained to teach other subjects as well. There is at present much call for teachers of ESL because of the numbers of refugees, immigrants, and foreign students coming to the United States. ESL teaching takes place also in high schools, colleges, adult education classes, vocational centers, and in special classes for refugees and immigrants.

Bilingual teachers should draw on the resources of the National Association for Bilingual Education (NABE), and ESL teachers will gain much help from belonging to TESOL, the association for Teachers of English to Speakers of Other Languages. (The addresses of these associations are listed in Appendix A.)

FOREIGN LANGUAGES IN THE ELEMENTARY SCHOOLS (FLES)

FLES became a nationwide educational phenomenon again in 1952, when Earl J. McGrath, United States Commissioner of Education, vigorously stressed the importance of foreign language study. There was an almost immediate response, and FLES programs were established throughout the country.

For those who want to teach foreign languages but who do not feel they can cope with some of the problems of secondary school teaching, FLES may be the answer. For many years, this concept meant introducing a foreign language into the elementary classroom for several hours a week through elementary conversation, games, and songs. Too often, however, such programs suffered from lack of integration into an extended program. At times the instruction depended largely on one or two individuals who often commuted between two or three schools. Such programs often collapsed when individuals left the school for any reason. The budgetary axe often was the cause of the demise of elementary language instruction.

Once again there has been a turnaround in foreign language instruction at the elementary level. Not only is there an increase in demand for teachers of young children, but there are growing numbers of partial or total immersion programs in some states.

The *ACTFL Newsletter* (American Council on the Teaching of Foreign Languages) tells of some pioneering efforts in this area:

> Typically, children begin learning a second language in kindergarten and continue through sixth grade by which time they are functionally fluent in the foreign language as well as English. This bears out research findings that indicate languages are most effectively learned during the first ten years of life. The children study a regular elementary school curriculum, but their instruction and text materials are in the language being learned. In a total immersion program, everything is taught in the second language in kindergarten through second grade, and youngsters rapidly learn a basic vocabulary of numbers, shapes, colors, letters, and other things that regular first and second graders learn. By third grade more of the instruction is in English, especially in such subject areas as art, music, and physical education in which specialized teachers probably don't know the second language. In partial immersion programs less instruction is given in the second language.

This level of language teaching seems to offer an area of employment for the future. Since children are generally able to learn a second language faster than adults, because they spend more time on the task, this trend could have significant effects when these students continue their language study at more advanced levels. Candidate teachers, however, are advised to inform themselves of opportunities in FLES or in immersion programs in the states in which they are interested in teaching before undertaking training; programs like these are not found in all areas of the country.

Apart from knowledge of the language and culture, it is essential that the FLES teacher be thoroughly trained for elementary school teaching and like working with young children. Many FLES teachers teach language only part of the time, and there is always the possibility of the program being phased out in a particular school district because of a changing educational or budgetary climate.

COLLEGE TEACHING

Professors at four-year colleges are usually expected to have completed doctoral programs and must continue to be productive in the three areas of teaching, research, and service to the college, and sometimes to the wider community. Most doctoral programs concentrate on literature, to a lesser degree on linguistics, and in a few institutions on the study of the culture of the native speakers or applied linguistics (theoretical aspects of language learning, with application to effective ways of teaching languages). Once the doctorate is completed and a position as assistant professor obtained, the new language and literature department member usually spends as much time on teaching language as on teaching literature or linguistics. With this in mind, a number of departments now ensure that all their doctoral students are well prepared to teach language. Some positions are available as language coordinators or language program directors, but for these positions applicants are usually preferred who have completed a doctorate in the linguistics of the language they will teach.

The initiation to college teaching is generally by way of the years of doctoral studies. Language department graduates usually support themselves through their studies by teaching undergraduates as teaching assistants (TAs) or Teaching Fellows (TFs). Fortunately for the undergraduate students in their classes, more and more universities are now providing their TAs with a course on the theory and practice of language teaching, a practicum on teaching techniques, and critiqued classroom supervision, often with videotaping of the novice teacher in action. This training improves the future teacher's chances of employment. With a slowly growing emphasis on the importance of providing language courses with an interdisciplinary emphasis (for example, languages for business, engineering, international affairs, or the health professions), future college professors of language should seek courses in which the young trainee may gain experience. The future teacher of language also needs broader knowledge than that provided in the typical language and literature department to be able to teach such interdisciplinary courses.

In some instances, native speakers without bachelor's degrees are hired if they can teach a rare language for which there are few qualified teachers. These positions are usually part-time, not well paid, and do not provide for professional advancement. For the more commonly taught languages, some instructors are hired as adjunct personnel to cover courses where there are not enough permanent instructors; these part-timers are usually expected to have the equivalent of a master's degree. Again these positions are not highly paid, and employment can vary from semester to semester or be abruptly terminated should there be an unexpected drop in enrollments. (Expected median earnings of college graduates with a bachelor's degree only in foreign languages and linguistics is $32,200, according to the *Occupational Outlook Quarterly,* winter 1994–95.)

At two-year colleges, some instructors will have doctorates, but others may be employed with master's degrees if they have experience teaching language in high schools. In some states, instructors are required to have teaching certification. The teaching load is frequently heavier than that at four-year colleges. The demands for research and publishing are less stringent, and salaries are generally lower.

College language teaching can be very exhilarating, as the teacher observes students develop a fascination with a new language and facility in using it. Frequently this experience culminates in accompanying study-abroad groups to a country where the language is spoken. These trips give the instructor the satisfaction of observing students' excitement in encountering a new culture within which they can communicate and form friendships—sometimes lifelong ones.

PROFESSIONAL ASSOCIATIONS

African Language Teachers Association
  Department of Anthropology and Linguistics
  Baldwin Hall
  University of Georgia
  Athens, GA 30602

America-Mideast Educational and Training Services, Inc. (AMIDEAST)
  1717 Massachusetts Avenue NW
  Washington, DC 20036

American Association for Applied Linguistics
  Suite 211
  1325 Eighteenth Street NW
  Washington, DC 20036

American Association of Teachers of Arabic
  4072 JKHB
  Brigham Young University
  Provo, UT 84602

American Association of Teachers of French
  57 East Armory Lane
  Champaign, IL 61820

American Association of Teachers of German
  #104, 112 Haddontown Court
  Cherry Hill, NJ 08034

American Association of Teachers of Italian
    Department of Romance Languages
    Wayne State University
    Detroit, MI 48202

American Association of Teachers of Slavic and East European Languages
    Foreign Language Department
    Arizona State University
    Tempe, AZ 85287

American Association of Teachers of Spanish and Portuguese
    Mississippi State University
    Mississippi State, MS 39762

American Association of Teachers of Turkish
    Near Eastern Studies
    110 Jones Hall
    Princeton University
    Princeton, NJ 08544

American Council for Collaboration in Education and Languages (ACCELS)
    1776 Massachusetts Avenue, NW
    Washington, DC 20036

American Council of Teachers of Russian
    5th Floor
    1619 Massachusetts Avenue NW
    Washington, DC 20036

American Council on the Teaching of Foreign Languages, Inc. (ACTFL)
    6 Executive Plaza
    Yonkers, NY 10701

American-Scandinavian Foundation
    725 Park Avenue
    New York, NY 10021

American Translators Association
    109 Croton Avenue
    Ossining, NY 10562

Association for Asian Studies, Inc.
  1 Lane Hall
  University of Michigan
  Ann Arbor, MI 48109

Association of Departments of Foreign Languages (ADFL)
  10 Astor Place
  New York, NY 10003

Association of Teachers of English as a Second Language
      National Association for Foreign Student Affairs (NAFSA)
  1860 Nineteenth Street, NW
  Washington, DC 20009

Association of Teachers of Japanese
  Japanese Program, Hillcrest
  Middlebury College
  Middlebury, VT 05753

Center for Applied Linguistics
  1118 Twenty-second Street NW
  Washington, DC 20037

Centre for Information on Language Teaching and Research
  Regent's College, Inner Circle,
  Regent's Park, London
  NW1 4NS, UK

Centre International D'Etudes Pedagogiques
  1, avenue Léon Journault
  92311 Sèvres, France

Chinese Language Teachers Association
  East Asian Studies Department
  211 Jones Hall
  Princeton University
  Princeton, NJ 08544

College Language Association (CLA)
  Clark Atlanta University
  James P. Brawley Drive at Fair Street SW
  Atlanta, GA 30314

Computer-Assisted Language Learning and Instruction Consortium (CALICO)
104 Lang Building
Duke University
Durham, NC 27706

Consortium of Teachers of Southeast Asian Languages
Foreign Service Institute
1400 Hay Boulevard
Arlington, MA 22209

Council on International Educational Exchange
205 East Forty-second Street
New York, NY 10017

ERIC Clearinghouse on Languages and Linguistics
Center for Applied Linguistics
1118 Twenty-second Street NW
Washington, DC 20037

Foundation for European Languages and Educational Centres U.S.A.
101 North Union Street
Suite 300
Alexandria, VA 22314

French Embassy Cultural Services
972 Fifth Avenue
New York, NY 10021

French Institute/Alliance Française
22 East Sixtieth Street
New York, NY 10022

German Academic Exchange Service/Deutscher Akademischer Austauschdienst
(DAAD)
930 Third Avenue
New York, NY 10022

Goethe Institute—Goethe House New York
1014 Fifth Avenue
New York, NY 10028

Instituto Italiano Di Cultura
    686 Park Avenue
    New York, NY 10023

International Association for Learning Laboratories (IALL)
    Humanities Learning Center
    Macalester College
    1600 Grand Avenue
    St. Paul, MN 55105

Joint National Committee for Languages
    Suite 211
    300 I Street NE
    Washington, DC 20002

Latin American Studies Association (LASA)
    9th Floor
    William Pitt Union
    University of Pittsburgh
    Pittsburgh, PA 15260

Middle East Studies Association of North America
    University of Arizona
    1232 North Cherry Avenue
    Tucson, AZ 85721

Modern Greek Studies Association
    Box 1826
    New Haven, CT 06508

Modern Language Association of America (MLA)
    10 Astor Place, 5th Floor
    New York, NY 10003

National Association for Bilingual Education
    Union Center Plaza, 39th Floor
    810 First Street NE
    Washington, DC 20002

National Association of Professors of Hebrew
    Department of Jewish Studies
    5800 Fulton Avenue
    Los Angeles Valley College
    Van Nuys, CA 91401

National Association of Self-Instructional Language Programs (NASILP)
    Center for Critical Languages
    Temple University
    Anderson Hall, 022-38
    Philadelphia, PA 19122

National Clearinghouse for Bilingual Education
    1118 Twenty-second Street NW
    Washington, DC 20037

National Council for Languages and International Studies
    Suite 211
    300 I Street NE
    Washington, DC 20002

National Federation of Modern Language Teachers Associations (NFMLTA)
    1933 North Fountain Park Drive
    Tucson, AZ 85715

National Foreign Language Center at the Johns Hopkins University
    4th Floor
    1619 Massachusetts Avenue NW
    Washington, DC 20036

National Resource Center for Translation and Interpretation
    School of Languages and Linguistics
    Georgetown University
    Washington, DC 20027

Russian and East European Language and Area Center
    Indiana University
    Ballantine Hall 565
    Bloomington, IN 47405

Teachers of English to Speakers of Other Languages (TESOL)
    1600 Cameron Street
    Alexandria, VA 22314

GOVERNMENT AGENCIES

Agency for International Development
  Recruitment, Office of Personnel
  320 Twenty-first Street NW
  Washington, DC 20523

Foreign Service Recruitment Division, Department of State
  Box 9317–Rosslyn Station
  Arlington, VA 22209

Central Intelligence Agency
  Director of Personnel
  Washington, DC 20505

Chamber of Commerce of the U.S.
  International Department
  1615 H Street NW
  Washington, DC 20061

Defense Intelligence Agency
  Civilian Personnel Branch
  Recruitment Section
  The Pentagon
  Washington, DC 20301

Defense Language Institute
  Foreign Language Center
  Presidio of Monterey, CA 93944

Department of the Air Force
Central Overseas Rotation and Recruiting Office
The Pentagon
Washington, DC 20330

Department of the Army
The Pentagon
Washington, DC 20301

Department of Commerce
Bureau of the Census
Washington, DC 20233

Department of Commerce
Bureau of International Commerce
Washington, DC 20230

Department of Defense
Office of Dependents Schools
2461 Eisenhower Avenue
Alexandria, VA 22331

Department of Education
400 Maryland Avenue SW
Washington, DC 20202

Department of Justice
Immigration and Naturalization Service
425 I Street NW
Washington, DC 20536

Department of Labor
Manpower Administration
Washington, DC 20210

Department of State
Language Services Division
Washington, DC 20520

Department of Treasury
U.S. Customs Service
Washington, DC 20229

Drug Enforcement Agency
    1405 I Street NW
    Washington, DC 20537

Federal Bureau of Investigation
    10th Street and Pennsylvania Avenue NW
    Washington, DC 20537

National Security Agency
    Office of Employment
    Ft. Meade, MD 20755-6000

Peace Corps
    Office of Personnel
    Room P-304
    806 Connecticut Avenue NW
    Washington, DC 20202

United Nations Headquarters
    Director of Personnel
    1 United Nations Plaza
    New York, NY 10017

U.S. Civil Service Commission
    Office of Personnel Management
    1900 E Street NW
    Washington, DC 20415

U.S. Customs Service
    Treasury Department
    1301 Constitution Avenue NW
    Washington, DC 20229

U.S. Information Agency
    Room 602
    301 Fourth Street SW
    Washington, DC 20547

World Bank Group
    Personnel Department
    1818 H Street NW
    Room D-1252
    Washington, DC 20433

APPENDIX C

PERIODICALS

Canadian Modern Language Review/Revue Canadienne
des Langues Vivantes
Ontario Modern Language Teachers Association
237 Hellems Avenue
Welland, ON L3B 3B8
Canada
(quarterly)

Champs-Elysées
P.O. Box 158067
Nashville, TN 37215
(14 times/year)

First Language
Alpha Academic
Halfpenny Furze
Mill Lane, Chalfont Street Giles
Buckinghamshire, HP8 4NR
England
(3 times/year)

Foreign Language Annals
American Council on the Teaching of Foreign Languages
6 Executive Plaza
Yonkers, NY 10701-6801
(bimonthly)

The French Review
  P.O. Box 149
  Chapel Hill, NC 27514
  (bimonthly)

German Quarterly
  American Association of Teachers of German
  112 Haddon Towne Court
  Suite 104
  Cherry Hill, NJ 08034
  (quarterly)

*Hispania: A Journal Devoted to the Interests of the Teaching
    of Spanish and Portuguese*
  American Association of Teachers of Spanish and Portuguese, Inc.
  University of Southern California
  Department of Spanish and Portuguese
  Los Angeles, CA 90089-0358
  (quarterly)

IRAL: International Review of Applied Linguistics in Language Teaching
  Julius Groos Verlag
  P.O. Box 102423
  Hertzstrasse 6
  D-6900 Heidelberg 1
  Germany
  (quarterly)

Italica
  Department of French and Italian
  618 Van Hise Hall
  University of Wisconsin
  Madison, WI 53706
  (quarterly)

Language Testing
  Cambridge University Press
  40 West Twentieth Street
  New York, NY 10011-4211
  (twice annually)

The Modern Language Journal
University of Wisconsin Press
Journals Division
114 North Murray Street
Madison, WI 53715
(quarterly)

Reading in a Foreign Language
Ray Williams & Alexander Urquhart International Education Center
College of St. Mary and St. John
Demford Road
Plymouth PL6 8BH
England
(twice annually)

Russian Language Journal
Michigan State University
A-601 Wells Hall
Department of Linguistics and Languages
East Lansing, MI 48824
(3 times/year)

Second Language Research
Edward Arnold Publications, Ltd.
Journals Department
42 Bedford Square
London WC1B 3SL
England
(twice annually)

Studies in Second Language Acquisition
Cambridge University Press
40 West Twentieth Street
New York, NY 10011-4211
(quarterly)

TESOL Quarterly: A Journal for Teachers of English to Speakers of Other Languages and of Standard English as a Second Dialect
TESOL Central Office
1600 Cameron Street
Suite 300
Alexandria, VA 22314
(quarterly)

BIBLIOGRAPHY

The works listed below are not intended as a complete or scholarly compilation of materials on foreign language study. They are merely a listing of some practical publications that may be of help to you in planning a foreign language career.

RECOMMENDED READINGS

Benjamin, Medea. *Peace Corps and More: One Hundred & Twenty Ways to Work, Study, and Travel in the Third World.* Santa Ana, CA: Seven Locks Press, 1991.

Bluford, Verada. "Working with Foreign Languages," *Occupational Outlook Quarterly,* Winter 1994–95, pp. 24–27.

Bourgoin, Edward. *Foreign Languages & Your Career,* 4th revised edition. Guilford, CT: Audio-Forum, 1993.

Carland, Maria Pinto and Daniel H. Spatz, Jr. *Careers in International Affairs.* Washington, DC: School of Foreign Service, Georgetown University, 1991.

Directory of American Firms Operating in Foreign Countries, 3 vols. A World Trade Academy Press Publication. New York: Uniworld Business Publications, Inc., 1994.

"The Foreign Language Needs of U.S. Based Corporations," Carol S. Fixman, in *Foreign Language in the Workplace,* 1990.

Foreign Policy Association, ed. *Guide to Careers in World Affairs,* 3rd edition. Manassas Park, VA: Impact Publications, 1993.

Gish, Jim, ed. *Civil Service Career Starter.* New York: Learning Express, 1997.

Goldenkoff, Robert and Dana Morgan. *Federal Jobs for College Graduates.* New York: Prentice Hall, 1991.

Hammer, Hy. *Civil Service Handbook.* New York: Macmillan Reference USA, 1998.

Krannich, Ronald L. and Caryl Rae Krannich. *The Almanac of International Jobs and Careers.* Manassas Park, VA: Impact Publications, 1991.

Krannich, Ronald L. and Caryl R. Krannich. *The Complete Guide to International Jobs & Careers.* Woodbridge, VA: Impact Publications, 1990.

Krannich, Ronald L. and Caryl R. Krannich. *The Complete Guide to Public Employment.* Woodbridge, VA: Impact Publications, 1990.

Lambert, Richard D., ed. *Foreign Language Policy: An Agenda for Change,* in The Annals of the American Academy of Political & Social Science, vol. 532. Newbury Park, CA: Sage Publications, Inc., 1994.

Lambert, Richard D., ed. *Foreign Language in the Workplace,* in The Annals of the American Academy of Political & Social Science, vol. 511. Newbury Park, CA: Sage Publications, Inc., 1990.

Lauber, Daniel. *Government Job Finder.* River Forest, IL: Planning/ Communications, 1997.

Lay, David and Benedict A. Leerburger. *Jobs Worldwide.* Manassas Park, VA: Impact Publications, 1996.

Moore, Zena, ed. *Foreign Language Teacher Education: Multiple Perspectives.* Lanham, MD: University Press of America, 1996.

Occupational Outlook Handbook, 1996–97. U.S. Government Printing Office. Washington, DC: U.S. Department of Labor, 1996.

Overseas Employment Opportunities for Educators. Alexandria, VA: Department of Defense Dependent Schools, 1996.

Padilla, Amado, M., Halford H. Fairchild, and Concepcion M. Valadez, eds. *Foreign Language Education: Issues and Strategies.* Newbury Park, CA: Sage Publications, Inc., 1990.

Rivers, Wilga M. *Teaching Languages in College: Curriculum and Content.* Lincolnwood, IL: NTC Publishing Group, 1992.

Rudman, Jack. *Foreign Service Officer.* Syosset, NY: National Learning Corporation, 1994.

Seelye, H. Ned and J. Laurence Day. *Careers for Foreign Language Aficionados & Other Multilingual Types.* Lincolnwood, IL: VGM Career Horizons, 1992.

Will, Cantrell and Francine Modderno. *How to Find an Overseas Job with the U.S. Government.* Oakton, VA: Worldwide Books, 1992.

GENERAL JOB SEARCH BOOKS

Adams, Robert L., ed. *The Adams Resume Almanac.* Holbrook, MA: Adams Publishing, 1994.

Beatty, Richard H. *175 High-Impact Cover Letters,* 2d edit. New York: John Wiley & Sons, Inc., 1996.

Beatty, Richard H. *The Perfect Cover Letter,* 2d edit. New York: John Wiley & Sons, Inc., 1997.

Bolles, Richard Nelson. *The 1997 What Color is Your Parachute?: A Practical Manual for Job-Hunters and Job-Changers.* Berkeley, CA: Ten Speed Press, 1996.

Fry, Ron. *Your First Job,* 2d edit. Franklin Lakes, NJ: Career Press, 1996.

Jackson, Acy L. *How to Prepare Your Curriculum Vitae.* Lincolnwood, IL: VGM Career Horizons, 1997.

Krannich, Ronald L. *Change Your Job, Change Your Life: High Impact Strategies for Finding Great Jobs in the 21st Century,* 6th edit. Woodbridge, VA: Impact Publications, 1996.

Krannich, Ronald L. et al. *Dynamite Resumes: 101 Great Examples and Tips for Success,* 3rd edition. Woodbridge, VA: Impact Publications, 1996.

Krantz, Les. *National Business Employment Weekly Jobs Rated Almanac,* 3d edit. New York: John Wiley & Sons, Inc., 1995.

Krantz, Les. *The World Almanac Job Finder's Guide 1997.* Hightstown, NJ: K-III Reference, 1996.

Larson, Jackie and Cheri Comstock. *The New Rules of the Job Search Game: Why Today's Managers Hire . . . And Why They Don't.* Holbrook, MA: Bob Adams, Inc., 1994.

Lauber, Daniel. *Professional Job Finder.* River Forest, IL: Planning/ Communications, 1997.

Marcus, John J. *The Complete Job Interview Handbook,* 3d edit. New York: HarperPerennial:HarperCollins, 1994.

McKinney, Anne, ed. *Resumes and Cover Letters That Have Worked.* Fayetteville, NC: PREP Publishing, 1996.

Petras, Kathryn and Ross Petras. *The Only Job Hunting Guide You'll Ever Need.* New York: Poseidon Press, 1994.

Wright, John. *The American Almanac of Jobs and Salaries, 1997–98,* rev. edit. New York: Avon Books, 1996.

Yate, Martin. *Knock 'Em Dead 1997: The Ultimate Job Seeker's Handbook,* 10th edit. Holbrook, MA: Bob Adams, Inc., 1996.

TRAVEL, STUDY, AND EXCHANGE PROGRAMS

Academic Year in Spain
  74 Little Neck Road
  Centerport, NY 11721

ACCELS
  American Council of Teachers of Russian
  1619 Massachusetts Avenue, 5th Floor
  Washington, DC 20036
  (High school exchanges, Russia)

American Council for International Studies
  19 Bay State Road
  Boston, MA 02215
  (Student travel)

American Field Service International
  Intercultural Programs
  313 East Forty-third Street
  New York, NY 10017
  (High school student exchange)

American Institute for Foreign Study
  102 Greenwich Avenue
  Greenwich, CT 06830
  (High school study, home-stay)

American Intercultural Student Exchange
  7728 Lookout Drive
  La Jolla, CA 92037
  (High school study, home-stay)

American Youth Hostels
  P.O. Box 37613
  Washington, DC 20013
  (Travel—Membership in AYH is necessary in order to have access to youth
    hostels of other nations.)

Amigos de las Americas
  5618 Star Lane
  Houston, TX 77057
  (Student work/service)

Amity Institute
  P.O. Box 118
  Del Mar, CA 92014
  (Foreign interns in United States)

Association of American Programs in Spain
  Department of Foreign Languages and Literatures
  Boston University
  Boston, MA 02215

AYUSA International
  151 Union Street
  San Francisco, CA 94111
  (High school study, home-stay)

Bike Europe (Publishers of *Budget Europe)*
  234 Nickels Arcade
  Ann Arbor, MI 48104
  (Travel)

Board of Foreign Scholarships
  Fulbright Program Exchanges
  U.S. Information Agency
  Washington, DC 20547
  (Study, exchange)

Council on International Educational Exchange
205 East Forty-second Street
New York, NY 10017
(Travel, exchange)

EF Institute for Cultural Exchange
1 Memorial Drive
Cambridge, MA 02142

Educational Foundation for Foreign Study
1528 Chapala Street
Santa Barbara, CA 93101
(High school study, travel)

The Experiment in International Living
Kipling Road
Brattleboro, VT 05301
(Exchange)

Federal Ministry for Youth, Family & Health
Kennedyallee 105-107
5300 Bonn-Bad Godesberg
Federal Republic of Germany
(Publishers of a booklet entitled *International Youth Meetings,* a valuable
source of information on numerous agencies that run international work
camps throughout the world.)

Franco-American Committee for Educational Travel
683 Fifth Avenue
New York, NY 10022

Future Farmers of America International Programs
National FFA Center
5632 Mt. Vernon Highway
Alexandria, VA 22309
(Work exchange)

German Academic Exchange Service (DAAD)
950 Third Avenue
New York, NY 10022
(Study, exchange)

German-American Chamber of Commerce, Inc.
    666 Fifth Avenue
    New York, NY 10103

German-American Partnership (GAPP)
    Goethe House New York
    1014 Fifth Avenue
    New York, NY 10028
    (Exchange, high school)

Ibero-American Cultural Exchange Program
    13920 Ninety-third Avenue NE
    Kirkland, WA 98033
    (High school study, home-stay)

Institute of International Education
    809 United Nations Plaza
    New York, NY 10017
    (Study, travel)

Interexchange
    356 West Thirty-fourth Street, 2nd Floor
    New York, NY 10001

International Association of Students in Economics and Business Management
        (AIESEC)
    841 Broadway, Suite 608
    New York, NY 10003
    (Traineeship exchange)

International Camp Counselor Program
    356 West Thirty-fourth Street, Suite 330
    New York, NY 10001

International Christian Youth Exchange
    134 West Twenty-sixth Street, Department CS
    New York, NY 10001

International Communication Agency
    Washington, DC 20547
    (Foreigner exchange in United States)

International Exchange Association
  1825 I Street NW, Suite 475
  Washington, DC 20006

International Student Exchange
  P.O. Box 840
  Fort Jones, CA 96032
  (Home-stay, high-school age)

International Travel Study
  4200 Fourth Street N
  St. Petersburg, FL 33703
  (Student exchange)

Nacel Cultural Exchanges
  3460 Washington Drive #109
  St. Paul, MN 55122
  (Home-stay, high school)

National Registration Center for Study Abroad
  823 North Second Street
  Milwaukee, WI 53203
  (Coordinating center)

Rotary International
  1560 Sherman Avenue
  Evanston, IL 60201
  (Exchange)

School Exchange Service
  National Association of Secondary School Principals
  1904 Association Drive
  Reston, VA 22091
  (High school home-stay exchanges)

Spanish Heritage
  116-53 Queens Boulevard
  Forest Hills, NY 11375
  (High school home-stay exchange)

Student Letter Exchange
215 Fifth Avenue SE
Waseca, MN 56093
(Pen pals)

Teacher Exchange Branch
United States Information Agency
301 Fourth Street SW
Washington, DC 20547

Trans-European Student Programs
P.O. Box 1485
Jamestown, ND 58402

Youth for Understanding
International Student Exchange
3501 Newark Street NW
Washington, DC 20016
(Exchange)